AMAZING STORIES

RATTENBURY

AMAZING STORIES

RATTENBURY

The Life and Tragic End of BC's Greatest Architect

HISTORY/BIOGRAPHY

by Stan Sauerwein

PUBLISHED BY ALTITUDE PUBLISHING CANADA LTD.
1500 Railway Avenue, Canmore, Alberta T1W 1P6
www.altitudepublishing.com
1-800-957-6888

Extreme care has been taken to ensure that all information presented in
this book is accurate and up to date. Neither the author nor the
publisher can be held responsible for any errors.

Publisher	Stephen Hutchings
Associate Publisher	Kara Turner
Editor	Audrey McClellan
Digital photo colouring	Scott Manktelow

We acknowledge the financial support of the Government
of Canada through the Book Publishing Industry Development
Program (BPIDP) for our publishing activities.

Altitude GreenTree Program
Altitude Publishing will plant twice as many trees as were used
in the manufacturing of this product.

National Library of Canada Cataloguing in Publication Data
Sauerwein, Stan, 1952-
Francis Mawson Rattenbury / Stan Sauerwein

(Amazing stories)
Includes bibliographical references.
ISBN 1-55153-981-0

1. Rattenbury, Francis Mawson, 1867-1935. 2. Architects--British
Columbia--Biography.* I. Title. II. Series: Amazing stories
(Canmore, Alta.)

NA749.R3S28 2003   720'.92   C2003-910578-4

An application for the trademark for Amazing Stories™
has been made and the registered trademark is pending.

Printed and bound in Canada by Friesens
4 6 8 9 7 5 3

The front cover shows Francis Rattenbury as a young man.
(Reproduced with permission from the City of Victoria Archives)

For the dreamers who risked.

Contents

Prologue

Alma watched as her cigarette slid away in the current. The River Avon barely seemed to move, but beyond the three arches of the railway bridge, near where she sat, she knew it mixed gently with the sea. It was inevitable. Just like this moment.

Relaxing in the fragrance of the wild iris blossoms that surrounded her, she caught sight of someone on the bridge. He stared, probably wondering how she had managed to navigate through the mud and bulrushes to get to the riverbank.

She had been on the train to Bournemouth from London, intending to see her boys. At Christchurch she suddenly realized they wouldn't be home. Villa Madeira was empty now.

In the fading light, she pictured Stoner in his cell, waiting for the noose, and slowly began to write.

"It must be easier to be hanged than to have to do the job oneself," she scrawled. "I tried this morning to throw myself under a train at Oxford Circus. Too many

people about. Then a bus. Still too many people about. One must be bold to do a thing like this."

She set the pen and paper down, picked up a dagger, then purposefully marched into the water. With a last look towards the bridge, she stabbed her left breast again and again. On the sixth thrust the dagger's blade sliced her heart.

Chapter 1
Chosen for Greatness

Vancouver offered everything an ambitious young dreamer could hope for as the world turned towards the 20th century. It was a city only sensing its future. Everyone living there was bent on wrestling riches from its wilderness. They were creating something momentous from the mountainous landscape, and to do it they needed factories, warehouses, churches, and homes. They wanted monuments to their achievements, and they needed architects to build them.

For a young man like Francis Mawson Rattenbury, Canada's West Coast was truly pregnant with promise.

Rattenbury

He was artistic and handsome, with a shocking red mane that hinted at his temperament. Gifted with imagination and talent, he was channelled into the family architectural business under the watchful eye of his bachelor uncle in Bradford, England. However, the firm's glory days were long over, and Rattenbury, chronically ambitious, dreamed of doing grand things. The tedious future his uncle painted for him once he became a full member of the Bradford firm didn't fit that image. The young man was confident, almost to a fault, and after five years in training he was certain there was nothing else his uncle could teach him about architecture.

He also knew that if he wanted a challenge, if he wanted to make his own mark, it would have to happen elsewhere. While he apprenticed, drafting plans for commercial and institutional projects, Rattenbury devoured stories in the London press about British Columbia. The chance of becoming part of this new country's dream pulled him like iron to a lodestone.

So in the spring of 1892, a tall and dashing young Rattenbury set sail for Canada. When he climbed from the transcontinental express at the Canadian Pacific Railway (CPR) station in Vancouver, his first sight of the city of 14,000 gave him both a shock and a thrill.

He knew Vancouver had only officially been called a city since 1886, so he expected to find a frontier settlement, but the haphazard collection of wooden two- and three-storey buildings on the shores of Burrard Inlet was the antithesis of centuries-old England. There were no Gothic cathedrals with their spires vaulting high above carved porticoes, no neatly defined cobblestone streets lined with structures designed to withstand the test of weather and time. Of the few substantial buildings that dotted the landscape of clapboard, Thomas Sorby's chateau-style CPR hotel was decidedly the most prominent.

Regardless of appearances, though, Rattenbury was excited by the splendid destiny of the place. He was positive he had made the right decision in leaving Bradford. British Columbia seemed to be the perfect place for a brilliant young architect to prove himself, and the 25 year old took his future success for granted.

After settling in at a boarding house, Rattenbury promptly turned to the task of establishing himself in his new land. He knew the first problem for an unknown British immigrant suddenly dumped in the hurly-burly of boomtown Vancouver was simply getting noticed. In solving that problem, Rattenbury discovered a talent for self-promotion he didn't know he had. Particularly when it came to advancing his ideas, Rattenbury's skill at doctoring the facts was shameless.

He announced himself in the newspaper, telling a

reporter he had spent "ten years erecting all classes of buildings in conjunction with the well-known firm of Lockwood and Mawson."

His statement was riddled with falsehood. It was true that Lockwood had been a partner in his uncle's firm when it designed Bradford's new town hall, but Lockwood died when Rattenbury was just 11 years old. Simple math would also have shown Rattenbury could not possibly have had 10 years' experience. Not unless he had started designing buildings when he was 15 years old. The newspaper reported it anyway.

Rattenbury conveniently failed to mention his one brush with early fame. He had received the Sloan Medallion in 1890 for his design for a public day school. The award, organized under the auspices of the Royal Institute of British Architects, was awarded to students and articled architects after a national competition. His plan was published in the *British Architect*, a prestigious industry magazine, but admitting to that award would only have prompted questions about the breadth of experience he was cleverly trying to claim.

The same day Rattenbury described his past successes, the paper carried a notice to architects announcing a competition for the design of new legislative buildings in Victoria. This was just the kind of structure he had come to Canada to build. Along with

66 other entrants from across Canada and the US, he hurriedly submitted sketches of the symbolic showpiece he sensed the government would want to build. He might have been working from memory, or perhaps his inspiration was simply the result of his training, but the sketch he submitted bore a striking resemblance to designs his uncle's firm had prepared years earlier for another architectural competition in England. Nonetheless, the young architect's own creativity was evident in the bold lines and beautiful form.

To ensure that no favouritism was shown in selecting a winning design, the two independent judges required architects to send in their entries anonymously. One submission was signed "Hopeful"; another, "Patience." Rattenbury saw a way to use this rule to boost his entry into the list of five semi-finalists.

He knew the competition would draw designs from many respected firms, but he also suspected the government would want to hire a local designer if at all possible. To improve his odds, Rattenbury signed his sketches "B. C. Architect."

His strategy worked. That November, Rattenbury was informed his sketch had made it into the finals along with another British Columbian, one from a Toronto firm, and three from the United States. Obviously he was selected as a finalist because of his design scheme, but his signature may have helped. His entry was a beautiful mixture of grandeur and practicality. With turrets and a central dome, the structure's ornamental features drew the eye. It was a building that demanded to be noticed.

Excitedly, Rattenbury dived into the job of enlarging and polishing his design. He had plenty of time. His announcement in the newspaper had attracted only one commission, for a small residence.

Pushing his luck with the nom de plume strategy just a little farther, Rattenbury decided to set himself apart from the American and Toronto entries in the same way again. He submitted a fine set of drawings for the final competition signed "For Our Queen and Province" to show he was not only a local architect, but also a British subject.

By way of a telegram on March 15, 1892, less than a year after the Yorkshireman arrived in Vancouver, Rattenbury learned he had won the most important architectural commission in BC history. The judges called his design a marvellous blend "of Romanesque, Classic and Gothic" influences. It was a perfect approach for a monument to British Columbia's growing economic stature, and one that the government was eager to show off. W. S. Gore, the deputy chief commissioner of lands and works, asked Rattenbury to come to

Victoria immediately.

It didn't take long for him to act. The day after he was informed he had won, Rattenbury moved into Victoria's finest hotel, the recently built Driard House. This was probably a small perk Rattenbury gave himself to celebrate, because he soon found less expensive accommodation in a boarding house on Menzies Street.

Before arriving in Victoria, he prepared an impressive statement of his credentials for the press, which was eager to introduce the winner to the world. "When he began the profession of architecture he entered the office of his uncle, Richard Mawson — the firm being the well-known one of Lockwood and Mawson of Bradford, England. This firm was one of the seven chosen out of all England to compete for the great Law Courts in London, and they it was who built the grand Town Hall of Bradford and most of the other great public buildings of the town. They built the whole of the model town of Saltaire — churches, mills, universities and markets. On many of these Mr. Rattenbury worked, after having served his articles for six years, gaining great practical experience from them."

His precisely crafted statement, which appeared in the *Vancouver Daily World* of March 18, 1893, demonstrates Rattenbury's opportunistic instincts. It was a carefully woven cloak of half-truths and outright deception, sewn to leave the impression of grand accomplishments without directly claiming personal credit. The law court competition preceded the day he joined his uncle's offices by 20 years. The Saltaire work began prior to his birth and ended before he arrived at the firm. Bradford's town hall officially opened when Rattenbury was just six years old.

But it was a forgivable deception. After all, Rattenbury quite rightly suspected the government might change its mind about entrusting the enormous sum of $600,000 to a 25 year old who had never handled a project of any magnitude.

Owing to Rattenbury's self-promotion, and the beauty inherent in his design, the press and government accepted his credentials without question. No one had the slightest worry Rattenbury might have trouble managing or completing the project, least of all the sublimely confident Rattenbury himself.

Chapter 2
A Job Well Done

Perhaps a seasoned architect would have had an easier time.

Within a month of his interviews by the newspapers, Rattenbury managed to complete his working drawings for the legislative buildings at a table in the boarding house where he stayed. To get the contract signed, however, he had to go to the construction trades with specifications, a difficult task. The sheer size of the project exhausted the local supply of building materials and qualified labour. Because of that shortage, the contractors inflated prices, and the lowest bid received was $17,000 more than the budget. The next lowest was $61,000 over the budget. It was submitted by a local builder named Frederick Adams.

In early December 1892, Rattenbury met with the province's chief commissioner of public works, F. G. Vernon. Rather than argue for more budget and give an impression that he was unable to keep the project's costs within the terms of the contract, Rattenbury attacked the problem from the completely opposite direction. He told Vernon he thought the legislative buildings could be built for less than the $600,000 the government had allotted. In fact, he said, a final figure closer to $550,000 could be possible if he reduced the quantity and quality of materials that were to be used.

Vernon was impressed and satisfied with this approach. However, to live up to his boast, Rattenbury had to tighten the screws on the trade contractors. He told Frederick Adams that he would have to shave his costs in order to get the contract. Adams may have inflated his estimate a little to improve his profit, because he had no trouble dropping his price. He recklessly agreed to a fixed price, and both men seemed pleased with the result of the contract negotiations. That peaceful arrangement did not last long.

The contractor's high estimate was a sign of things to come. Over the course of the project, the government was faced with cost overruns that amounted to almost

$400,000 more than it had budgeted. (The politicians may have expected this to happen and possibly viewed the project as a way to boost the depressed Victoria economy.)

In part the overruns were Rattenbury's fault. He had the habit of changing his design on the fly. Correcting oversights in his plans, the young architect would sometimes order alterations to work already finished, or he would add construction elements that were not budgeted in the original design. A good example of this was the matter of stone selected for the construction.

When it came time for the stonemasons to start work, Rattenbury made a change. He rejected the entire shipment of stone received for the project from the Koksilah quarry. After inspecting it at the job site he turned it back, supposedly because it was damaged.

The contractor was horrified. The stone Rattenbury was rejecting was material the architect had handpicked at the quarry the winter before. Regardless, Rattenbury told the contractor that he judged the stone to be imperfect and that he worried about the building's stability if it was used. Critics — and Rattenbury had many among the jealous architects in Victoria — later claimed he didn't notice the colour was wrong when he first placed his order. They alleged that by rejecting the stone, he was simply covering up for a mistake. The

Rattenbury

The legislative buildings in downtown Victoria

criticism may have been at least partly justified. Months later, John Teague, another architect in the city, used the rejected stone to build the Jubilee Hospital without a problem.

The accusations of mistakes didn't faze Rattenbury. He was arrogant and stubborn on the matter and he forced the contractor to get new stone from a second quarry on Haddington Island, even though it cost 50 percent more. He also demanded that Adams absorb the extra cost because of his agreement to a fixed price for the job. This was devastating to the contractor's projected profit. Worse still, the stonework on the south side of the building ended up costing double the original estimates because of changes Rattenbury arbitrarily ordered while it was being built.

The construction was a nightmare for the contractor. As the costs added up he was pushed towards bankruptcy, and when he reached the point at which he could not pay his workers, he was finally forced to give up the contract. Rattenbury didn't seem to care. Angry and frustrated at the way he had been treated, Adams turned to the government, complaining that his financial predicament was all Rattenbury's fault. He demanded compensation and claimed an inquiry into the matter would prove Rattenbury had caused the collapse of his company.

Because of the public nature of the legislative buildings project, the government had no choice but to comply. True to his adversarial nature, Rattenbury welcomed the opportunity to argue his case. At the public hearing into the matter, both men were openly hostile to each other, hurling accusations like schoolboys in a fistfight.

The dispute was a tremendous embarrassment to the government. Ultimately, it could hardly support the unfortunate contractor in the dispute without leaving politicians open to criticism over the selection of the design and the architect. Rattenbury was able to rely on his overblown "credentials." Though the government was appalled at the serious clerical errors that were discovered in Rattenbury's accounting, it supported his management. To the contractor's dismay, it even paid a $3000 bill Rattenbury submitted for his time attending the meetings.

On March 22, 1895, not long after the hearings, a tragic sailing accident handily put an end to the contractor's complaints. On a weekend excursion out of Victoria Harbour, Adams fell overboard and drowned.

About 18 months after Adams' sailing accident, new contractors completed the stonework for the legislative buildings, and Rattenbury acted as if the dispute had never happened.

Government bureaucrats in the public works

department did not forget the embarrassing incident, though. They pressured Rattenbury to make design changes to save money on the project. In December 1893, Rattenbury had said he could save $44,000 by omitting marble and stained glass from the Domical Hall and the Legislative Hall. In November 1895, the newly appointed public works commissioner, G. B. Martin, asked Rattenbury for the savings. The architect objected. He claimed that "no future expenditure, however large, could in any way compensate for the omission, and the amount, in comparison to the cost and character of the buildings, is comparatively small, considering the marvelous improvement it would effect."

Martin relented, realizing the rotunda and legislative hall were probably the building's finest features, but he was back at Rattenbury again in the spring of 1897. He demanded the east pavilion, an area that had been destined to house the Land Registry, become a museum, with the Mining Bureau laboratories in the basement. Rattenbury argued repeatedly against the museum and laboratory notion. His written complaints were long and intemperate, and he finally convinced Martin to reconsider his ideas for the mining bureau but not the museum.

Then, without consulting Rattenbury, Martin obtained his colleagues' approval to relocate the museum to the main floor of the east pavilion and ordered fixtures for the museum. On learning of Martin's covert activity, Rattenbury sent another indignant letter to the commissioner. In it he dramatically offered his resignation.

"Believe me," he wrote to the commissioner, "much as I would regret to sever my connection with the Parliament Buildings especially after having for so many years exerted every faculty and made such painstaking endeavours to carry out the works to as perfect and satisfactory a conclusion as possible, still, I am ready to resign my position as Architect of the Buildings a position no longer tolerable, if not accompanied by confidence, and so afford you the opportunity of obtaining other professional advice and assistance."

Rattenbury's resignation was resisted with arguments that the architect must proceed on the project, but only with the permission of the commissioner. Rattenbury managed to curb his temper.

While the bureaucrats desperately tried to seize control of the project, Rattenbury cunningly got them bickering amongst themselves over who was in charge. The battle over supplies and ordering procedures resulted in a constant stream of arguments and accusations. Rattenbury always managed to sidestep any problem with his wit and his showmanship.

One incident illustrates Rattenbury's ability to

skewer even the most powerful bureaucrat. In November 1897, Martin refused to pay the contractor who was laying the sidewalk at the legislative buildings because the work had not been approved by the works department.

That December, the architect wrote to Martin to say he had ordered the sidewalk at the behest of the premier. "There certainly seems to be a little confusion in these various mandates," he said rather sarcastically, implying that Martin was not the supreme authority and that Rattenbury took his direction from the top.

Despite his fights with the bureaucrats, work on the legislative buildings went ahead successfully. The east wing was finished on September 19, 1896, and the politicians were using the legislative assembly in 1897. Of course, by then the squabbles no longer mattered to Rattenbury. He had completed the monumental project in style, and it officially opened on February 10, 1898. The fame it brought him inflated his ego.

His attitude of self-congratulation and superiority was obvious in a letter he wrote to his mother on November 14, 1900, describing the project and his role in it. He was extremely proud of his accomplishments and considered the government's interruptions only an annoyance.

"It used to be such great enjoyment to me when we

were building the Parliament Buildings, to take it easy in the cool shade and watch a couple of hundred men pounding away for dear life on the hard stone." One can easily imagine Rattenbury, relaxed in a comfortable chair with his plans unrolled in front of him, presiding over the construction mayhem.

That the young man managed to finish a project of such complexity without formal experience says a great deal about Rattenbury's grit and vision. He produced a structure more impressive than any of his contemporaries imagined, a building that everyone in the province could point to proudly. It was, and continues to be, a monument to British Columbia's shining future. Without his arrogant attitude, and his courage to risk, it would not exist today.

The *Victoria Times* applauded the architect as a brilliant visionary and the buildings as a stunning achievement. It gushed that Rattenbury had managed to blend three styles into one building, "not a jumble by any means, but an adaptation and modulation to the general effect in a masterly and artistic whole, pleasing to the eye yet not sacrificing the utilitarian purposes which public departments demanded...The beauty of the structure calls forth the admiration of everyone who has seen it, while the perfection of the work and the thoroughness in design and in choice of the stone for the buildings, the good taste and judgment displayed, has been decidedly happy, the result being a harmonious picture delightful to the eye."

In an even more glowing compliment a few years later, the future King George V cited the BC legislative buildings and the Ottawa parliament buildings as two of the finest examples of architecture in the Dominion at that time.

In the rush to congratulate anyone who had taken part, the newspaper accounts overlooked the building's glaring deficiencies. No one mentioned, for instance, that the acoustics in the legislative assembly were so poor that workmen had to hang fishing nets from the ceiling to break up the echo so speakers could understand each other. Or that the press gallery did not include desks for reporters to write on. Or that the lieutenant-governor's suite of rooms on the third floor, used for formal government functions, did not have washrooms.

Those inconveniences were minor mistakes. The province was agog and celebrated in high style when the legislative buildings were opened. Everyone was pleased and ready to heap honours on the architect, but Rattenbury was nowhere to be found. He was already chasing a new dream with the considerable wealth he had gathered from his commissions.

Chapter 3
The Klondike Risk

The young Yorkshireman was careful with his money. On August 25, 1894, he wrote to his uncle, Richard Mawson, to describe his life since he had arrived in Canada. He had earned commissions of $40,826.07 from the legislative buildings job, an enormous sum that would exceed $833,000 today.

"I have steadily invested my money in the safest securities I could find," he wrote, "now and then putting $100 in a speculation, just on a chance." As it turned out, one of those speculations was the Klondike gold rush.

On July 17, 1897, when the steamer *Portland* docked

in Seattle and offloaded 68 passengers and more than two tonnes of gold, there were few people in Victoria who even knew the Klondike existed. Within a few weeks, however, the strange-sounding name was on everyone's lips. The lure of Klondike gold, waiting to be scooped up by anyone who was enterprising and adventurous, caused every segment of society to contract gold fever in one way or another. Rattenbury was no exception.

During the winter of 1897, as the legislature project wound down, he found himself involved in the purchase of 60 head of cattle, which were delivered to Dawson City. A more philanthropic sort might have provided the beef to the hungry miners for a reasonable profit, simply out of concern for their lives. Not Rattenbury. After a perilous expedition to Dawson, the cattle arrived during a terrible winter at a time when most residents were on the verge of starvation. Rattenbury took quick advantage of the situation and sold the cattle for as much as $1000 a head.

The price he commanded was not out of line. While the miners had gold, there was not much to buy. Before the restaurants ran out of food, $5 in gold dust could buy a meal of beans, stewed apples, bread, and coffee. Miners could buy a pound of desiccated potatoes for a dollar or spend $3 on the same amount of rancid flour.

Rattenbury probably got the idea of a cattle drive to

the Yukon from cattle baron Pat Burns, who he met while designing buildings for the Bank of Montreal in BC's Kootenay region. In 1896, Rattenbury had been hired to design the bank's office in Victoria. The result, in a French-chateau style, pleased the directors so much they hired him to design their banks in the province's Interior as well.

Pat Burns was a short, stout fellow who had earned his first fortune supplying fresh meat to railway workers building a line from Regina to Prince Albert, Saskatchewan. An enterprising man with a good nature and even disposition, he expanded his business to Alberta and then the BC Interior. Burns established a headquarters in Nelson and was supplying fresh meat to Rossland, Greenwood, Kaslo, and other places in the Kootenays when Rattenbury arrived.

Knowing miners in the Klondike needed meat, Burns had previously bought 85 head of cattle and shipped them to Skagway from Vancouver. The cattle were driven over the White Pass in August and then overland to the Yukon River. Once there, they were slaughtered. The freshly butchered quarters were tied to rafts built on-site and floated to Dawson.

But the Yukon River could be treacherous. Loaded and top-heavy as they were, several rafts were lost in the swirling rapids along the way or smashed on the rocks.

The Klondike Risk

It was obvious a safer method of transportation was needed if any scheme to supply beef to Dawson was to work efficiently.

That gave Rattenbury an idea.

He decided a fleet of shallow-draft riverboats, large enough to shoot the Five Finger Rapids 400 kilometres from Dawson, would solve everyone's problems.

In the first week of February 1898, while plans for the opening of the legislative buildings were the talk of the town, Rattenbury was trying to put his idea into action. With a partner, a City of Victoria clerk named Wellington J. Dowler, he headed off to England aboard the Atlantic steamer *Lucania*. The two intended to attract investors willing to risk a little cash for a big pay-off. Their plan met with quick success and raised £75,000 to finance Rattenbury's transportation scheme.

Rattenbury returned to Victoria and began work. He decided to have the boats built there and shipped to Skagway. Upon arrival they would be carried, in pieces, by pack horses all the way to Lake Bennett.

This lake, at the headwaters of the Yukon River system, was where men and women en route to the Klondike stopped after their arduous trek from Skagway, lugging a year's worth of supplies over the White or Chilkoot passes. The gold seekers usually rested a while on the windy shores before preparing for the final leg of their journey. They chopped down trees and used whip-saws to cut the timber into boards. Many had no experience building boats, so the makeshift craft they made were often hard to steer. Navigating them down the lake and through the waiting rapids was a dangerous and often fatal task.

Instead of setting up his operation where he might encourage competition, Rattenbury secretly established a mill 40 kilometres down the lake. The boat parts he shipped on horseback were then put together at the mill, neatly out of sight. In the spring of 1898 his first steamer was being constructed.

By May he had signed a $40,000 contract with Pat Burns to ship more cattle to Dawson using the vessels that would be operated by his Bennett Lake and Klondyke Navigation Company. Refusing to let even the slimmest chance for profit escape, Rattenbury included passenger accommodation in the design of his boats, though he knew the men and women who struggled to reach Lake Bennett had often used up their life savings buying supplies for their Klondike adventure. They could not pay for a ride on the final leg of their trek, but the well-heeled businessmen arriving to service this flood of miners would.

Using his influence and reputation, Rattenbury skillfully promoted his transportation solution to the wealthy in Victoria. He was in his element when talking about his project with prospective business customers at the Union Club or in the swirl of Victoria society engagements.

While Rattenbury socialized, his mind was not entirely focused on business. He was a handsome, wealthy bachelor and an intriguing lure to marriage-minded Victoria debutantes. He might easily have picked a wife from among the attractive, educated daughters of powerful men, but for some reason he didn't find any of them marriageable. Perhaps his conservative upbringing played a part in it. He may have been looking for a stable and quiet relationship with a woman who would be less challenging or demanding.

In any event, as he launched his northern fleet, he also embarked on matrimony. Not much is known about how Rattenbury met the woman who became his first wife. During the construction of the legislative buildings, the chief commissioner of lands and works conducted his business from Eleanor Howard's boarding house, a little bungalow opposite the cathedral on Rae Street. Rattenbury was required to make regular visits there, and that is probably how he first met Florence Eleanor Nunn.

Up to then, Florrie had led a simple, and in many ways a sad, life. Her father, George Elphinstone Nunn, was a retired British Army officer who arrived in Victoria with his wife and children in 1862. He had been attracted by the news of a gold rush on the Fraser River, but when he got to British Columbia he discovered the gold rush was already spent. Rather than find work in Victoria, he signed on with a coastal freighter that plied the route between Victoria and San Francisco and left his wife to raise their brood alone. He returned now and then over the years, fathering more children, including Florrie, but then came home no more.

After years waiting for him, Florrie's mother learned that her husband had died in San Francisco. She struggled to rear their children by herself, without financial support. When she got the news of his death, she packed her bags and left for Portland, Oregon, to live with one of her older daughters, who had married into a wealthy family. Her daughter and her daughter's husband must not have wanted the entire family. Florrie's brother Charles was sent to a farm in Saanich, and Florrie, less than 10 years old, was left in the care of the widow Howard.

Florrie was hardly the catch that a Victoria debutante might have been for ambitious young Rattenbury. She had little money and tried to lift her low social status by claiming she was related to the distinguished Elphinstone family, which had played a major role in

Florrie

the history and government of British India. Her connections to that family were dubious. She was also homely and short, with a prominent nose and square jaw. Her eyes were large, almost frog-like, but while her physical charms may not have been captivating, she did have other admirable qualities. She was known for being kind to everyone she encountered, and she displayed a patient serenity in everything she did.

Rattenbury must have seen those other qualities and fallen in love with Florrie because of them. Perhaps her quiet, servile nature attracted him as well. With domestic skills gained at the boarding house, she was an ideal homebody. She was no doubt closer in nature to the memories he had of his mother than were the pampered Victoria socialites he met so often. Rattenbury, who had proven to be extremely tight with his money, might also have seen some value in marrying a woman more inclined to thriftiness than extravagance.

While work proceeded at a fast clip on his Bennett Lake and Klondyke Navigation Company, he courted Florrie and made sketches of a little cottage by the sea, the home he planned to build for his new wife. When he was about to launch the first steamer, Rattenbury proposed to Florrie.

The 31 year old, who was practically an old maid by the standards of the time, happily accepted. The two were married at Christ Church Cathedral on June 18, 1898, in a quiet ceremony attended by only a handful of friends and Rattenbury's brother. The circumstances of their tiny wedding seem contrary to Rattenbury's normally flamboyant way of doing things. Florrie may have been "in the family way." Their first child was born only seven months after their wedding.

If the wedding was out of the ordinary for Rattenbury, the honeymoon was not. He turned it into a business trip to the Klondike via Dyea, Alaska.

Chapter 4
Northern Honeymoon

For anyone without money, getting to the Klondike was a trial of will and courage. Lake Bennett, where Rattenbury sited his mill, was reached by climbing over either the White Pass or the Chilkoot Pass. At the summit of each the North-West Mounted Police waited with scales, ready to turn back anyone who did not have at least one year's worth of supplies.

The distance from Dyea, Alaska, to Lake Bennett over the Chilkoot was 56 kilometres. In winter, the first 21 kilometres followed a frozen creek bed to Sheep Camp. This was where stampeders cached their supplies before taking on the pass. They carried their goods in packs on their backs, 35 kilograms at a time, from Dyea to Sheep Camp. Transferring all their possessions could take 35 or 40 trips. By the time they were ready to tackle the Chilkoot, they had already walked more than 1100 kilometres.

At Sheep Camp the real work began. The stampeders now had to move their supplies another 6 kilometres uphill. There they faced a 35-degree climb up the "Golden Stairs." Twelve hundred steps had been hacked in the frozen snow, and the stampeders walked them, groaning under the weight of their packs, time and time again. They did it in a flowing sort of rhythm that became known as the Chilkoot Lock-Step. They were like links in a chain that draped down the mountainside. It was so steep that a man could drop to his knees on the climb and still seem to be almost upright.

Once a man started his ascent up the Stairs, there were only two places where he could step out of line and rest. The first was a large, overhanging boulder called the Stone House. The second was the summit.

Although a single trip was not a problem, doing it over and over was a terrible ordeal. Many never went another step towards the gold fields around Dawson. Those who did carry on after the excruciating climb arrived at Lake Bennett exhausted and often penniless.

Many wrote home afterwards to describe the tortuous journey, and the frightening stories did a good job of discouraging others of fainter heart from attempting the trek.

Rattenbury, ever conscious of the need for promotion, did his best to paint a different picture. Only a week after his marriage, in a letter to an employee in Victoria named E. T. Potts (who he obviously knew would pass the missive along to the *Victoria Colonist*), he described their trek over the Chilkoot Pass much differently: "There were really no difficulties on the trail. We simply strolled along and actually did not know that we had come to the dreaded part of the Pass until we were told that we were at the summit. You can judge by this how ridiculous and exaggerated the accounts we have read of it must have been."

Rattenbury did his best to entice more stampeders. In the correspondence he claimed Florrie found walking about in Victoria more tiring than "strolling" the Chilkoot. It was an unspoken challenge to any man who read the news and worried about the trip. Rattenbury as much as said that if a frail woman could do it, anyone could.

Others, though, had chilling accounts of the trek. Martha Louise Black, who crossed the pass two weeks later, reported the climb nearly killed her. "I was straining every nerve, every ounce of physical endurance in that upward climb. There were moments when, with sweating forehead, pounding heart, and panting breath I felt I could go no further.

" — stumbling — staggering — crawling — God pity me!

"Another breath! Another step — God give me strength. How far away that summit! Can I ever make it?"

Rattenbury and Florrie left Dyea at 4 o'clock on Friday afternoon and arrived at Lake Bennett by 6 o'clock the following evening. They spent the night on the shore before moving to the mill camp. Once there they were treated to a well-prepared camp of five tents, complete with front terraces. It was a far cry from the flimsy lean-to structures that the exhausted stampeders built for themselves a little farther around the lake.

"The climate is delightful, cool and fresh," he wrote to Potts. "I have not yet seen a single mosquito...We are all in capital health and spirits, and shall probably stay here about a fortnight, taking the run down to Dawson and back in the meantime."

Rattenbury proudly supervised as Florrie christened the third steamboat to leave his mill. He had named all three after her — the *Ora*, the *Flora*, and the *Nora*. However, he changed his mind about visiting Dawson because of the amount of work he had organizing things on Lake Bennett and because of the time the journey would have added to his stay.

Dawson was said to be the largest city west of Chicago and north of San Francisco, with 40,000 people wildly clawing for the riches of the Klondike. Lots were selling for as much as $5000 per front foot. Prospectors, eager to enjoy their wealth, were trading gold dust for everything from French champagne to withered carrots, at highly inflated prices. From the stories he was told, the wily architect estimated the profits to be made from his transport business at nothing short of enormous!

His optimism received a serious shake on the trip home, however. In a letter to Otto Partridge, a man he had employed with his brother Jack to run the Lake Bennett mill, Rattenbury described a much different return journey.

"Of all the men I was the most miserable. I tried riding, the trails were too rough. I tried walking, it was just as bad. Some stretches of the trail were so nauseating, owing to the carcasses of dead donkeys, mules and horses that it overcame me. I could simply not stand it. In the higher latitudes the mosquitoes were scarce, thanks to a breeze blowing. How on earth the packers managed it is past my comprehension. Asking them how they could put up with it day after day, they said, 'Oh, we thrive on it. It saves us a meal once in a while.' I could not see anything to joke about. Of the two evils, mosquitoes on the Mclintlock, or the Skagway trail, I could make no choice. I must have taken a fever for several days until nearing Victoria. I was sick, which was something new to me. Carry on up there! I can now understand how so many men died on those putrid trails, and know what you have to contend with. I'll remember you. Everything is in your hands."

But business was business to Rattenbury, and telling the truth at all times was not one of his virtues. Though he had been ill on the boat back down the coast to Victoria, he managed to improve enough by the time they docked to put on a smiling and energetic face. To ensure even the most cautious stampeder would be willing to make the journey north, he proudly informed onlookers that he and Florrie were returning on a ship that also carried $20,000 in gold from the Klondike. It served as exciting proof of the potential gold seekers would be passing up by staying at home.

He assured everyone that development of the Klondike would follow the rush. To bolster the claim, he reported that a railway was already being built over the White Pass from Skagway to Bennett. It would make the trip no more than a pleasant holiday.

Rattenbury's assessments were naïve. He did not realize that the gold rush stampede was quickly spiralling to a trickle. An estimated 100,000 people had charged north, but most had arrived too late. By the time they got there, the best claims were already taken. The stampeders wandered about Dawson aimlessly, wondering what to do with themselves.

And unknown to Rattenbury, as winter approached, many of the defeated and frustrated were returning to their homes in the South. Luckily, no one else in Victoria realized it either. He managed to raise $100,000 in just two days from eager investors so he could address the problem of travel in the Klondike during winter. On August 19 the *Victoria Colonist* reported that Rattenbury had formed a new business called the Arctic Express Company. In fact, Rattenbury had used his investors' money to purchase a company headquartered in Seattle that had already been working on the problem.

His plan, he told investors, was to build a string of relay stations, 50 kilometres apart, from Lake Bennett to Dawson. They would allow travellers to make the trek during the winter in comfort and safety. He promoted his system of relay stations by saying it was "second in extent and completeness to none in the world, not even excepting the famous Siberian relay."

It was a shrewd purchase for Rattenbury considering the AEC came with an $80,000 annual contract already secured to carry the US mail between Dawson and the coast. But by October the company was in trouble.

Although he had built the relay stations as promised, bought sled dogs, and hired the staff, his idea fell apart almost immediately. To make the trip from Dawson to Skagway required one thing he could not supply. Snow.

Without snow, he had no travellers. He couldn't even move the mail. The bad luck of cold, clear weather eventually forced Sam Steele and his North-West Mounted Police to take on the mail delivery themselves when Rattenbury's company failed in its attempts. The AEC lost the postal contract.

Even more distressing was the fact that most of the people still left in Dawson were heading in the opposite direction by that time. From the moment he purchased the assets of the AEC, passengers and freight had dropped drastically. Rumours were quickly spreading of a new gold strike farther north at Nome, Alaska.

When spring arrived, Rattenbury's boats were ready to ply the lake and river, but there was little to transport and lots of competition. By the time summer turned to autumn, more than half of Dawson's population had moved to Nome.

Rattenbury's scheme was not working, no matter what sort of spin he put on the situation. To save face, he pulled back from his Bennett Lake and Klondyke Navigation company, claiming his architectural business demanded too much of his time.

While they may have grumbled, his investors probably realized Rattenbury had lost a fortune of his own money, as well as theirs, on the failed scheme. The AEC continued to operate for a time, with Rattenbury listed as its Canadian agent, but it never fulfilled his dream.

His detractors saw Rattenbury's attempt to run a transportation company in the North as a failure. In fact, it had great symbolic importance. He showed that fairly speedy transportation was possible in the North. With his intervention, the trip from Victoria to Dawson took only nine days: four days on the steamer to Alaska; one day on the trail; and three or four days aboard steamers on the Yukon River system.

In spite of his northern disappointments, Rattenbury's reputation as the province's premier architect remained intact. At the end of the year he was embarking on new projects for one of the nation's powerhouse companies — the Canadian Pacific Railway.

And he was a father.

Chapter 5
Rescued by CPR

Friends happily welcomed Florrie and "Ratz" back to the cultured atmosphere of Victoria, and the couple moved into an elegant residence rented from the manager of the Victoria branch of the Bank of Montreal. The architect did all he could to make the failure of his transportation empire a quickly receding memory. He settled into the less arduous pace of a privileged life in Victoria, once again embracing the social swirl and regularly hosting friends and business associates at the Union Club.

He also actively sought new architectural work and

promoted himself into commissions of all sorts, including the rebuilding of Cary Castle — the lieutenant-governor's home — which had been destroyed by fire.

Once again, envious competitors roundly criticized the way he manipulated the situation to get the commission. First he worked as an advisor to the government, claiming he was too busy to look at the job himself. When another architect was selected, Rattenbury offered a negative evaluation of the projected costs. Even though the government was still in dispute with him over clerical irregularities for the legislative buildings, he was asked to take on building the new residence. Showing a firm grasp on human nature, Rattenbury successfully gained control of the purse strings.

His habit of constant design changes during construction had not changed. As well, during the Cary Castle project he was busy with several other buildings simultaneously, and his accounting of what materials went with what job left much to be desired. Hounded by those who wished to see him taken to task on the matter, he was criticized for ordering goods not included in the budget and even sliding some purchases into his own home project.

Rattenbury thrived on controversy in public, though, at least outwardly, his private life appeared happy and unaffected by it all. On January 14, 1899, Florrie gave birth to their first child. Sadly, Francis Burgoyne Rattenbury was born with clubfeet so badly deformed that it was thought Snooka or Snookie, as he was nicknamed, would never be able to walk. Florrie naturally smothered the child with love. Despite having the appearance of a man who kept his emotions in check, Rattenbury doted on his son too.

The birth gave Florrie a reason to keep to herself. Life on fashionable Rockland Avenue was alien to shy, humble Florrie. She simply didn't fit into graceful Victoria society well. The wealthy women she had to befriend and socialize with on behalf of her husband never forgot her past. In their minds, she would always be the adopted daughter of a boarding house keeper with a brother who made his living as a waiter.

Amidst the bustle of activity surrounding the construction of Cary Castle, Rattenbury undertook to build his young family a home of its own. It was located on the beach in Oak Bay, and Rattenbury proudly adopted a native name for the place: "Iechinihl" (Eye-a-chineel). The house was built on the spot where Native legend said man was first given speech, and, literally translated, the name meant "the place where a good thing happened."

He described the name's meaning to his mother

in a letter written on May 30, 1900. "For centuries our particular garden has been an Indian camping ground...They had a legend that formerly all men were dumb and looked at each other like owls. But one day on this very spot the good spirit conferred on them the gift of speech."

Rattenbury's design for the home was a departure from traditional architecture in Victoria. It was compact and practical by mansion standards and looked like an adaptation on an English cottage, so it fit the area well. At the time, Oak Bay was a spot where Victoria's wealthy were building informal summer homes.

Florrie was instantly happy at Iechinihl, escaping her feeling of inadequacy. She tended a seaside garden in shy retreat and cared for Snooka. Rattenbury was not about to give up social contact entirely, however. He bought Florrie exquisite jewels to wear when guests appeared for their many summer parties. He filled the home with fine furniture and hired servants.

Life in Oak Bay was quiet and sedate for the family, but to the rest of Victoria, Rattenbury appeared as active as ever. When he had work to do he attacked it with gusto, and when it was finished he always felt the need to find more. His commissions ranged from Vancouver to the BC Interior and Alberta, and he was often writing to his mother or sister in England about uprooting his family and returning there to make life a little less hectic. He thought his hard-earned reputation in Canada would stand him in good stead if he worked from a headquarters in London. Besides, it would give him the chance to flit over to the Continent and travel, which he loved to do.

His intention to move took a back seat, however, when another plum appeared on the West Coast development horizon.

Canadian Pacific Railway (CPR) originally opened its Hotel Vancouver on May 16, 1887. The six-storey brick building underwent several additions over the years, but it was still not large enough to handle the increasing traffic of visitors coming to the growing city of Vancouver. In October 1900, Sir Thomas Shaughnessy, CPR president, announced the company wanted to demolish the old hotel and replace it with a 250-room version. Because of its size, the new hotel represented the most important architectural commission in the province since the legislative buildings. Rattenbury's eyes sparkled.

CPR went to a competition to select a designer, and he submitted his ideas, but admitted to his family he was not a shoo-in for the job. In fact, on December 18, 1900, he wrote to his mother to say "the architects of the East are pulling strings" and he was concerned about his chances. He shouldn't have been. In February 1901 he got the good news. His design had won.

He travelled to Montreal immediately to familiarize himself with the company's plans. By winning the competition, Ratz had been unofficially selected as CPR's western division architect. The chateau style of building he had provided for the Bank of Montreal was almost a trademark for the railway's tourism endeavours, so it appeared Rattenbury was the perfect choice for designer. As well as the Hotel Vancouver, he was asked to design a renovation to tiny Mount Stephen House at Field. CPR had plans to open that area to tourism, and guests would require a grander place to stay. He may also have learned that Sir Thomas Shaughnessy wanted a western bookend for his hotel business in Victoria as well.

Rattenbury was happy to oblige all the company's requests.

Back in Vancouver by February 19, 1901, he announced his plans to rebuild Vancouver's landmark hotel. The new facility, to be erected in stages, would cost between $400,000 and $500,000 — almost as much as the original contract for the legislative buildings, he proudly proclaimed. It would have 250 bedrooms when completed and would boast all the most modern of conveniences.

Suddenly, with other commissions rolling in, Rattenbury was too busy to even think about moving to England. He wrote to his mother on August 20, 1901, describing his workload. In the five months since his appointment, cutbacks at the railway company had reduced the budget for the Hotel Vancouver project to $300,000 but he had other jobs to deal with at the same time, including additions to the Jubilee Hospital, additions to the Victoria Courthouse, a mansion for Pat Burns in Calgary, and Cary Castle in Victoria. All considered, he would earn $104,000 in commissions that year (equal to more than $2 million today), an enormous income for an architect at the time. With all that work, Rattenbury finally had to break down and part with some of his cash to hire an assistant.

The Hotel Vancouver project became a long, unfinished process for Rattenbury. Construction of the western wing of the hotel began in December 1901. It was almost a year before workmen got the roof on and started plastering the interior. The new section was not completed until 1905. Aside from the refurbishing of the old hotel, this was the only part of Rattenbury's design to be erected. CPR may have decided to curtail the Vancouver project so it would have the funds it needed to build a new hotel in Victoria. Rattenbury could hardly complain.

The demands on him were tremendous. He spent most weekday evenings entertaining at the Union Club in Victoria. Florrie was left alone to putter about her Oak Bay hideaway with only servants and Snooka to keep her company. She reacted to having an absentee husband by withdrawing from Rattenbury and trying to gain some financial independence.

Always a penny-pincher, Rattenbury barely tolerated her attempts. On October 22, 1902, he wrote to his mother complaining about Florrie's almost juvenile mistakes at household budgeting. "She elected some time ago for an allowance to buy all her own necessaries. Now I find she was beguiled into getting jewellery at so much a month and her millinery bills consequently are mounting up. I am not supposed to know of the jewellery deal and she is trying to convince me that the allowance is too small and I ought to pay off outstandings and increase it. I ask for more information and to myself chuckle."

Besides Florrie's little intrigues, Rattenbury had other personal problems to deal with. Efforts to correct his son's clubfeet with special boots failed, so he decided to send Frank and Florrie to a surgeon in San Francisco, where he hoped the deformity might be corrected. Florrie's stay there stretched into months as Frank recovered. The separation did little to help their marriage. Rattenbury was also worried about his younger brother, who had left the Klondike after that business failure and moved to the Far East.

In spite of turmoil in his private life, Rattenbury continued using whatever spare time he had to expand his business reach. For one thing, he leveraged his newly invigorated reputation in hotel design in several ways.

In Victoria, the owners of the Hotel Dallas, near the city's Outer Wharves, invited Ratz to do for them what he was achieving for CPR. The latter company might have considered his taking on this commission while the Hotel Vancouver was being built a conflict, but when was the client ever in control of Rattenbury's career? He set to work on the Hotel Dallas and even started to entertain discussions with another competitor of the railway.

In November 1902, Charles Melville Hays, president of Canada's second oldest railroad, the Grand Trunk, announced he was planning to build a transcontinental line with a terminus on the northern Pacific Coast. Hays, like Rattenbury, was a man with a forceful personality. He declared the railroad would run through central British Columbia, along the Nechako, Endako, and Bulkley rivers to the Pacific. At the mouth of the Skeena, on a rocky outcrop called Kaien Island, he intended to build a new terminal city.

It seems every momentous project of the time started with a competition. This one, to find a name for the terminal city, attracted the interest of thousands of people, including Ratz. Eleanor MacDonald, niece of Manitoba's lieutenant-governor, submitted the winning entry. The terminal city, yet to be built, would be called Prince Rupert.

Exactly when Rattenbury started talking about Prince Rupert building requirements with Grand Trunk Pacific Railway (GTP) is uncertain. Some historians believe he may have became close to someone with confidential knowledge before 1907, because Ratz began the process of carefully buying up land along the likely route of the railroad. Others point out that Sir Sandford Fleming had undertaken a feasibility study of northern routes for CPR in the 1870s, and while a GTP route was not known, Rattenbury could easily have guessed it at.

The *Victoria Colonist* reported he made his first acquisition of 4451 hectares in the Nechako Valley as early as 1903. He also acquired land in the Bulkley Valley, property between Hazelton and Houston, and three parcels in the Fort St. James area north of Vanderhoof, spending a total of $150,000 by 1907.

The purchases used up the bulk of his savings. In

January 1908 he wrote to his sister Kate, telling her about his speculative investments and saying, "In five years though it will be worth five times as much, when the railway runs through, although I may not wait so long."

True to his word, he sold his Nechako Valley land for a reported $100,000, but then reinvested it in more property in the Nass Valley.

The gamble on the GTP left Rattenbury short of cash, but it seemed he was unstoppable as yet another landmark commission came his way.

Chapter 6
Dressing the Empress

and speculation was quite all right as far as Canadian Pacific Railway was concerned, and Ratz found himself learning from the masters.

CPR had its eye on Victoria as a port for expansion of its shipping empire. Secretly, it wanted to add to its network of tourist hotels as well. The company's strategists, however, were not about to spoil future profits or increase potential costs by revealing their intentions too early.

The railroad had purchased an aging fleet of 14 vessels from the Canadian Pacific Navigation Company in January 1901. That part of the plan was public and could not be denied. The company intended to upgrade its transportation network, including a passenger run between Vancouver and Victoria, but reports in an eastern newspaper claiming the company had definite plans to build a hotel in Victoria were flatly denied.

In June 1902, a month after Rattenbury finished renovating the Hotel Dallas, CPR president Sir Thomas Shaughnessy visited the city on one of his annual cross-country tours. Among his many scheduled appointments he agreed to meet with a Board of Trade committee and hear members press their case for a Victoria hotel like the stunning expansion project Rattenbury was doing for Vancouver.

The businessmen tried to convince the apparently uninterested railway baron that building a first-class hotel in Victoria made good economic sense. Victoria was destined to be a tourist mecca, they said. The temperate climate and beauty of the West Coast made that fact a given. What Victoria needed was a showpiece hotel.

The committee fawned and fussed with presentations. The gardens of James Douglas's former residence, close to the legislative buildings, might be a good location, members suggested.

Shaughnessy showed little interest. He told them

CPR did not want to expand its hotel business, and that was plain and simple. After hearing the committee's suggestions for locations, though, he admitted the presentation did offer some interesting possibilities. Shaughnessy's bait had been offhandedly cast to a pool of hungry fish.

The bait was jigged a bit more a day later when an unidentified source informed the *Victoria Colonist* that perhaps CPR might be interested in building a hotel on reclaimed land behind a newly built harbour causeway. The causeway had been constructed a year earlier to replace a dilapidated bridge that spanned tidal mud flats.

Determined not to give up easily, the committee worked to prepare information on three alternative sites for a possible CPR hotel, which it would present to Sir Thomas on his next visit. Among the sites was the causeway property. The mud flats were practically valueless to the City of Victoria, and the committee only added this property to its list as an afterthought.

Returning to Victoria in May 1903, Shaughnessy again graciously met with the committee. One more time he told them CPR was "very much averse to going any further into the hotel business."

But, he asked, if CPR did proceed, what cooperation could the company expect? The committee suggested tax exemptions might be provided if a hotel were built on the Douglas property. Shaughnessy replied that offer might sway his board of directors and then made a counterproposal involving the causeway land.

"If the city will supply the site and exempt us from taxation and give us free water for 20 years, we will build a hotel to cost not less than $300,000," he told them bluntly.

The committee was ecstatic. Rushing back to City Hall, members gathered plans for the James Bay flats and roused Rattenbury. Would he kindly sketch the ground floor of a hotel on this site to prove to Sir Thomas it would be suitable for a CPR hotel? Ever the good citizen, Ratz said he would do his best. The next night, with amazingly detailed sketches in hand, the committee met with the CPR president again.

Located on 1.8 hectares, the hotel that Ratz had sketched was a five-storey building with 150 bedrooms. Shaughnessy studied the plan carefully before proclaiming that only a hotel of 250 rooms would be suitable on such a site. The committee had taken his bait.

Rattenbury's overnight "sketch" appeared in the newspaper the following day. No one stopped to question how a man, even one with Ratz's talent, was able to make such a detailed drawing so quickly. It showed the legislative buildings on one side, the post office and new Carnegie Library on the other, with a stunning hotel as a centrepiece of the harbourscape. There it was in glorious detail, sitting atop as yet unreclaimed land the committee had only recently considered a possible site.

Regardless of any manipulation by Sir Thomas, or Rattenbury's part in it, City Hall put its intention to sell the land and provide tax concessions to the voters. Rattenbury had to wait until June 8, 1903, when city council received notice of the final passage and assent of Bill 63, "The Tourist Hotel." He expected to be called to Montreal to discuss the plans for the hotel in detail at any time.

On June 14 he wrote to his mother, telling her he was not looking forward to that chore. "I am half-expecting that I shall have to go to Montreal again in two or three weeks, over the big hotel proposed for Victoria. I don't fancy the trip much in the middle of the summer. I much prefer basking on the shores of the Pacific Ocean at Oak Bay surrounded by myriads of flowers and with a nice cooling drink within reach and Snookie's prattle to keep me awake."

City council's plan to snag CPR was approved by an overwhelming majority of citizens, though exemption from water rates and taxes would only extend for 15 years. Nonetheless, congratulatory telegrams crisscrossed the country.

By December, Rattenbury had plans ready. He announced CPR would build a grand seven-storey hotel reminiscent of the Chateau Frontenac in Québec City. The hotel he envisioned would become a tourist attraction unto itself.

It would be "a picturesque castle effect of the French Renaissance school of architecture," he said, and would have an enormous entrance hall in "Old English style," to be designed without concern for cost. As well, there would be a glass-roofed palm garden decorated in a Chinese motif, and a massive dining room. To cap the announcement, Sir Thomas promised that CPR would transform the mud flats, once the city paid to fill them in, of course, into "the beauty spot of Canada."

Excitement over the project faded as progress dragged in the months that followed. More land had to be expropriated for the site. More concessions had to be wrung from the voters. It was nine months from the day Ratz unveiled his plans before construction of the first stage finally began.

Rattenbury's life, both personal and professional, continued on its complex course in the meantime. On December 27, 1903, he wrote to his mother, reporting on their family Christmas. "Florrie's shadow gets larger; I don't think she will be traveling this spring. We tell

Snookie he is going to have a brother called Nicolas, one of the old names."

On May 11, 1904, five years after their son Francis was born, Ratz and Florrie celebrated the birth of a second child. Mary was a beautiful girl, gifted with her father's blue eyes and erect carriage. However, like her brother, she too suffered a malady. A high-strung, nervous sort, she developed a bad speech impediment that may have been rooted in emotional trauma. It later become evident to friends and acquaintances that Rattenbury's quiet, private marriage to a wife who was becoming ever more stout might be in trouble.

But Ratz did not allow his personal problems to affect his public persona. He continued to build and to promote his activity with energetic dedication. Plans for the Victoria hotel underwent several revisions. The first course of bricks were not laid until August 1905. Because it had taken so long for the Victoria project to get rolling, Ratz decided to recharge the public's interest. In the middle of August he called for a competition to name the hotel. It had to happen soon, he told the press, because the hotel was due to open the following summer!

The public was eager to take on the challenge. The Hotel Van Horne, the Royal Oak, and the San Juan de Fuca were suggested, but finally CPR decided that only

The Empress Hotel today

the Empress, a title that fit so well with the regal name of its city, would do for such a fine hotel. City council, believing Rattenbury's prediction about completion, also revived its interest in the project and contracted to have 135,000 pamphlets printed extolling the virtues of Victoria and of the showpiece that was to be the Empress Hotel.

Rattenbury used the time before construction of the hotel began to compete for the design of a new

Vancouver Courthouse. In late February 1906, he wrote to his mother that he was almost finished and quite pleased with himself. "I am rather set up with them," he wrote, adding a sketch of the classical-style building into the margin. "It looks quite swagger, but I dare say there will be a swaggerer."

He was right. In August he was awarded the commission for what was to become a Vancouver landmark. He also won the commission for another courthouse in Nelson, and his style set a new standard for large courthouses in the province and for institutional architecture in Vancouver.

True to Rattenbury's history during this flurry of design, however, the construction of the Empress dragged on. When council criticized him for the delay, Ratz lashed back, blaming the city. He claimed the municipality had agreed to prepare the grounds for landscaping, but to that point had not done the job.

By November 1906, the predicted opening was 14 months overdue, but Ratz was unconcerned. In fact, with the arrogance for which he was famous, he ignored the rising public criticism of his missed deadlines and dropped a bombshell.

He had been cementing his relationship with the CPR's competitor. Now he proudly unveiled plans for another hotel, this one to be built by Grand Trunk

Pacific in Prince Rupert.

The $50,000 structure would be temporary, he advised, with the obvious certainty of a planning insider. It would remain open only until Charles Hays' new railway line was completed to the yet-to-be-created Pacific port. When that happened, said Rattenbury, a much larger and grander hotel — a facility even finer than the Empress — would be built from his designs.

Perhaps it was the public nature of this announcement that spelled the end of Rattenbury's relationship with CPR. Within a month of his proud public statements, a storm had begun to brew between Rattenbury and the CPR's chief architect, W. S. Painter. Eventually the bickering exploded into a dispute over interior décor planned for the Empress. Ratz issued another of his haughty ultimatums, perhaps believing his reputation as the province's premier architect would pull him through. The company could either follow his advice, he snapped, or it could find another architect.

Painter calmly chose to say good-bye. On December 5, 1907, the *Victoria Colonist* announced Rattenbury had resigned his commission for the Empress, stating as the reason the architect's unwillingness to change the location of the office in the hotel.

Rattenbury's ego was bruised when CPR accepted his resignation. The rejection smouldered within him, eroding any pride he felt for his accomplishments with the Empress. The blow was so deep, in fact, that he refused to attend the hotel's official opening on January 21, 1908.

By the end of 1907, Rattenbury had designed an almost new Hotel Vancouver; overseen the interior décor of a CPR steamer, the *Princess Victoria*; designed and supervised construction of the Empress Hotel; designed an addition to Mount Stephen House at Field; and been asked to prepare plans for an expansion of the Banff Springs Hotel. His resignation meant giving up the commission for that hotel as well.

With his design skills and voracious appetite for promotion, he had definitely made a mark on the company. He had also left an indelible impression on the province generally. His buildings had become significant landmarks from Vancouver to Nelson. It was obvious Rattenbury did not see the loss of the CPR commission as a career setback. The Empress was almost complete anyway, and the GTP plans to build Prince Rupert offered him new and spectacular challenges.

Rattenbury had no way of knowing world events would soon demolish the GTP's plans.

Chapter 7
Grave Errors

A fter the relationship with CPR turned sour, Rattenbury kept himself busy with a number of commissions to build houses for the well-to-do in Victoria. He also found himself attending to new elected duties for the residents of Oak Bay. The residents had formed the Oak Bay Improvements Association when Victoria refused to extend the city boundaries and include the community within them. Rattenbury had accepted a position as one of four councillors, along with James Herrick McGregor, William Oliver, and another architect and friend, Samuel Maclure.

In March 1908 Rattenbury left Canada for Britain and an extended trip to Europe. He probably wanted to console his mother over the recent death of his father. His mother had written to him in late February that she was ill too, plagued by gallstones.

When he returned to Victoria in June, he seemed revitalized. A motor tour of the Continent had spurred his interest in town planning. What he saw filled him with a new sense of urgency for Victoria. He began in earnest trying to convince the City Fathers that Victoria's economic future depended on tourism. He preached the need for municipal control of the design of buildings, imploring councillors to set aside land for city parks and playgrounds, and to form a board that could review all townsite plans.

What was needed, Rattenbury claimed, was the conviction to be creative. Banish uniformity, he said, and inject "some artistic taste."

Despite his reputation, Victoria's city council ignored him, allowing industrial development to sprout in some of the worst locations possible, including on the waterfront. A paint factory was located on Laurel Point, and enormous oil storage tanks on the other side of the harbour marred the views from the Empress.

Rattenbury was ready to champion Victoria's development with his modern ideas for public green space. Unfortunately, the boom in Victoria flattened. As development interest suddenly dropped, the architect found there was little he could do.

Professionally he kept busy in the spring of 1911 with another commission from the provincial government. This was to expand the legislative buildings to provide more offices, a parliamentary library, and new space for the provincial museum, the Government Printing Office, and a garage.

A series of arguments with the provincial librarian and archivist about design nagged him through this project, and no doubt Rattenbury was annoyed and fed up with bureaucrats. That summer he took Florrie to England to visit his mother one more time before she died. Through the years his mother had become his closest confidante, and he feared her loss a great deal. She had been a wellspring of affection and advice to which he turned often, and her passing later that year left a tremendous void.

In spite of the year's negative events, the future still held promise. He looked forward to the challenge of the Grand Trunk Pacific project. His earlier commission from GTP ranked second only to that which he earned with the legislative buildings.

Now the GTP's plans to build its own network of hotels to rival the CPR's, and the investments that were projected — as high as $4.5 million — gave Rattenbury ample reason to believe in rosier times ahead. The Prince Rupert hotel alone would be the most imposing tourism facility ever designed in the West. It was to have 450 rooms, with a dining room capable of seating 265 people. Twice the height of the Empress, it would tower over Rattenbury's dream of a garden city. He knew the project would be historic and profitable. His commissions on the $2-million structure would be enormous.

Seeing the wild success that CPR was having with the Banff Springs Hotel (during the summer of 1910 it was booked to capacity, and the following summer 22,000 visitors were registered), Charles Hays formally commissioned Rattenbury to design a string of hotels along the GTP line in the Canadian Rockies. Ratz picked Jasper, Miette with its hot springs, and the base of Mount Robson as sites.

Hays also planned a huge promotional campaign to entice tourists and extol the virtues of the rich farmland settlers would find along the route. This also made Rattenbury happy. The influx of customers Hays projected would be prospective buyers for Rattenbury's northern landholdings.

The following spring, however, Ratz faced the first of many disappointments concerning GTP.

Hays, who had travelled to England to meet with

shareholders and win coal export contracts, was among the victims who went down with the *Titanic*. While the company did not retreat from Hays' vision afterwards, the man who replaced him, E. J. Chamberlain, was considerably more cautious and less enthusiastic. GTP continued laying track as planned and, to match its progress, decided to build the Chateau Miette at Jasper and a hotel at Mount Robson from Rattenbury's designs.

To keep himself occupied while he waited for the projects to begin, Rattenbury decided to run for office. Perhaps still slighted by Victoria's failure to follow his advice on town planning, Rattenbury turned his attention to Oak Bay. He wanted to ensure the same unrestricted expansion he had witnessed in Victoria did not happen there, so he ran for the position of reeve.

In his election platform, he hinted at his objective: "I think that the Oak Bay district is one of the most lovely residential areas that I have ever seen, and it is my desire to retain this beauty as far as possible." He meant parkland and strict building guidelines and controls.

But being a defender of green space placed Ratz in the middle of a hotly argued debate. The local economy was in a slump and businessmen wanted development, no matter how it looked. In one of the hardest-fought elections Oak Bay had seen in years, Rattenbury managed to squeak into office on his planning agenda with a tiny majority of 24 votes.

While he should have been excited, it appears that Ratz was just the opposite. The economic slump made it impossible to sell bonds for parkland acquisition and a road-paving program he envisioned. He had a dream for Oak Bay and no way to achieve it financially. His frustrations with business and public life were beginning to show. At 45 years old, though he was still healthy and enjoying notoriety, his once fiery red hair was turning gray prematurely and his vigorous disposition was declining. At home he was often despondent about the pace of the Prince Rupert plans.

When the GTP's inaugural transcontinental express from Winnipeg arrived at Prince Rupert on April 9, 1914, Ratz finally had reason to be excited about work again.

Perhaps sensing a need to revitalize before he faced the challenges of the GTP's building program, Rattenbury planned another trip. He would take a cruise with his daughter Mary as a companion, he declared. Mary, however, declined. A trip without Florrie was unthinkable, she told her father. She would miss her mother too terribly and be poor company as a result.

Disappointed but not deterred, Ratz left for England alone. If he could not squire his daughter, he would spend time with his son, Frank, who had been enrolled in Wyllie's School at Hampstead Heath.

When Ratz arrived in August, Frank travelled to London to meet his father. While dining together on August 14, they heard the shocking news that Britain was declaring war on Germany.

His restful little trip, doomed from the beginning, quickly came to an end.

The two Rattenbury men immediately rushed back to Victoria. Though he had only been gone a short time, Ratz found a much different city, gripped by patriotic zeal. Everyone's mind was on war, not building.

Ratz, like most other able-bodied men, tried to enlist, but he was rejected immediately as too old. He would have to sit on the sidelines watching one of the greatest military clashes in history. As the war intensified, the rosy future he had imagined shaping in the development of the northern territories evaporated as the GTP hotel program collapsed.

Without the mental challenge of work or the social distraction at his club because so many members were in the war, Rattenbury had to settle for whatever joy he could make of life at home. This was a poor substitute because of his tattered relationship with Florrie. His wife's lack of social and intellectual skills became a burden for Rattenbury.

The couple no longer spoke to each other, communicating via notes only when absolutely necessary. Now, with Rattenbury constantly about the household, their relations worsened. By the middle of 1918 they decided to have separate bedrooms, and Ratz transformed his into a private apartment where he took his meals alone. Every evening he tackled the better part of a bottle of whisky. He wished to avoid having to interact with Florrie and "Grannie" Howard, who had by this time closed her boarding house and moved into their Oak Bay home.

In the same period, Florrie's relationship with her own family deteriorated as well. Her natural mother was destitute in Portland. In 1918, Florrie's sister, Mary Brenner, started legal proceedings to try to force Florrie to provide some support, but Florrie flatly refused any aid for the woman who had abandoned her. Her mother died in poverty the following year.

With his marriage a sham and his dream of a northern Eden filled with settlers building homes on the land he owned crushed by the war, Rattenbury was left only with hopes of selling his land to returning war veterans. Now these were suddenly stymied as well.

As the war looked to be ending, the BC government devised plans to provide returning soldiers with a chance to own land in undeveloped areas, just as Rattenbury had expected. There was heavy political pressure for the government to protect the veterans from land speculators, however. A Land Settlement Board was created to manage resettlement of the soldiers. The Board selected the Bulkley Valley as one of three areas in the province where they could be settled, and the chairman, Maxwell Smith, approached Rattenbury about buying his property. Though he and Smith worked out a purchase at two-thirds of the cost Rattenbury had originally paid for the property, other Board members later rejected the deal, calling most of his land worthless.

Instead of buying their land, the Board required owners like Rattenbury to improve their holdings within a specified time or face a tax levy amounting to 5 percent of the land's assessed value.

During October 1918, the Board approached him again. This time it offered Rattenbury a price that is suspected to have been far below the market value. Ratz decided he would try to improve the land instead. Privately, he had managed to sell 1800 hectares between April and October. He was working hard to find buyers for the rest, but the Board insisted on specified improvements to all his holdings anyway and warned him he would face the tax if he did not sell the land.

To protect himself personally, Rattenbury incorporated Rattenbury Lands Ltd. to assume ownership of his remaining property and energetically entered the real estate business. He became the sole agent for a number of other land companies and by February 1920 was appointed the Canadian representative of the Canadian Landowners' Association. The Association was a grouping of 20 British companies with landholdings in Canada.

Rattenbury travelled to Britain in July 1920, hoping to find a buyer, but he was not successful. In August he wrote to his daughter, telling her, "This is certainly one hard game I have set myself." Ratz stayed in London until early 1921, living in a $4-a-week room, constantly hunting for a saviour. In June, all his sales hopes collapsed.

That month the Land Settlement Board notified him that it was buying part of his land and the sale would be compulsory. In some cases the land had been appraised for less than the price at which it had already been sold to others. Those buyers, seeing the difference between the price they were paying and the assessment, walked away from their deposits. Ratz claimed that the Board's heavy-handed tactics had cost him $520,000, but it did not change matters. In fact, Rattenbury was served a tax notice on unimproved property for $90,000, to add insult to his financial injury.

He faced both professional and personal disaster because of his property in the north and became even more ill-tempered than he had been before.

But as was the case when his northern transportation scheme failed, architecture pulled him through again. That September, in a flash of post-war optimism, the Victoria Chamber of Commerce proposed the idea of a new civic swimming pool. Voters had turned it down nine years earlier, but the businessmen suspected the negative response was due to the crude designs that had been offered for the vote. This time, they decided, they needed the best design possible. Years before, Rattenbury had promoted the idea of a Coney Island-style recreation area for Victoria, so they lured Rattenbury out of his Oak Bay lair and asked if he would design them a pool.

Rattenbury seized on the assignment. In a burst of newfound energy, he produced sketches that were stunning in concept. The Chamber had requested a pool, but Rattenbury gave it an amusement centre. His sketches showed a facility with three heated seawater pools, towers, ballrooms, picture galleries, and shops, all topped by an enormous roof of glass.

While the Chamber canvassed for electoral support, Rattenbury did some hunting of his own. Though he was happy to provide the grand vision, he no longer wanted the tedious task of finishing the working drawings. He found an architect, Percy Leonard James, who was willing to produce them and supervise the construction if the amusement centre was ever built. Rattenbury threw himself into the project's promotion instead.

However, after Rattenbury and the Chamber spent two years beating the drum for the amusement centre, voters were still lukewarm on the idea. A by-law for the swimming pool didn't have the slimmest chance of passing, but miraculously, CPR stepped forward with a suggestion. Concessions it had enjoyed upon completion of the Empress had expired. Would Victoria be willing to provide free water for the pool for 20 years and freeze taxes on the hotel for the same length of time if CPR put up $200,000 to build the amusement centre?

The City Fathers enthusiastically responded "yes"! With Rattenbury as their eager front man, they flooded the city with handbills and speaking engagements. On nearly the last day of the year, a referendum for the amusement centre concessions passed with an overwhelming majority. No one bothered to check the numbers in the CPR's generous offer very carefully. The company would retain any admission profits from the pool and enjoy $750,000 in tax concessions in return for its altruistic $200,000 investment.

Nonetheless, the city was flushed with excitement. The community was about to have another architectural marvel after all. To celebrate after the December 29, 1923, amusement centre vote, local businessmen hosted a banquet at the Empress, with Rattenbury proudly listed as the guest of honour. Their cheers were wild and raucous.

Loud enough for a flamboyant young woman to take admiring notice.

Chapter 8
The Meddling Madonna

On December 23, 1923, Ratz wrote to his sister Kate. The government's action regarding his northern landholdings had been weighing heavily on him, but he was happy to report something new in his life. The previous evening he had been to a dance and met a young married woman named Alma Pakenham.

Only 26 years old, she was "the belle of the ball and a marvelous musician," he wrote. He seemed taken by the fact she had paid him a compliment he had not heard often before.

"You have almost the kindest face I ever saw," the

young woman had flatteringly told him.

She was a haunting beauty with a carefree smile and "bedroom" eyes, the kind of modern girl matronly socialites disapproved of because she drank cocktails and smoked cigarettes in public. Though she wore her hair bobbed short over her ears and sported shapeless, flapper-style dresses, the soft curves of her body could not be disguised. She was a creature of passion, self-absorbed and worldly — the opposite of staid, aging, and irascible Rattenbury.

Born in British Columbia about 1895, Alma Victoria Clarke was a musical talent who played both the violin and piano and had even been described as a child prodigy. She learned at an early age all about the sweet pleasure to be wrung from applause. As she grew up she was pampered and allowed tantrums her mother happily excused as artistic temperament. People fussed over her. As a result, Alma matured into a selfish fun-seeker, the kind of person who did as she pleased and was sometimes oblivious to the emotional consequences of her actions.

By the time Alma was 18, she already had gained a small portion of fame with her musical talent. She studied at the Toronto College of Music and had performed with the Toronto Symphony Orchestra.

In 1913, she was an attractive catch for Vancouver

real estate agent Caledon Dolling. If it hadn't been for World War I, her first husband might even have tamed her.

At the outbreak of the war, Dolling was given a commission and eventually shipped overseas to join the 2nd Battalion of the Royal Welsh Fusiliers, which was being sent to France. Madly in love with her young groom, Alma refused to be a "widow in waiting" in British Columbia. She followed him to London and took a job at Whitehall so she might be close by when he was granted leave.

Dolling was evidently a courageous soldier. After being wounded in February 1916, he received the Military Cross. Wounded again in April, he recuperated with Alma until July. Then he returned to the front just in time to die that August at the battle of Mametz Wood.

Widowed and devastated by her loss, Alma quit her job at Whitehall and joined the Scottish Women's Hospital Organization. It was a group totally composed of women — doctors and all. The British refused to have an "all-woman ambulance corps," but the French were less picky. Alma soon found herself serving in the French Red Cross at Royaumont and in the advance hospital at Villes Coltert. She showed a talent for nursing the wounded. For courage in the face of fire she received the Croix de Guerre from the French government.

During her service in France she met the man who would become her second husband. Thomas Compton Pakenham, a member of the family that holds the Earldom of Longford, shared Alma's love of music. Thomas was the nephew of widely admired Admiral Pakenham, and Alma apparently took to his arms with more than willing abandon. The social taboos she shattered by carrying on with a married man seemed to make little difference to her. Their relationship, fanned by her passionate nature, quickly caused the collapse of Pakenham's five-year-old marriage when the war ended.

In 1920, as soon as the divorce was final, the couple wed and left for New York where Thomas was to become the chief music critic at the *New York Times*. Alma gave birth to her first child, Christopher Compton. Their marriage was not a happy one, and within two years it was over.

With her mother's help, Alma whisked Christopher to Victoria, leaving Thomas behind forever. Back in BC, her mother encouraged Alma to resume the flowering musical career the war had forced her to abandon.

On the night of the banquet celebrating the amusement centre vote, Alma was in the Empress lounge with friends, relaxing after a recital.

Drawn by the loud chorus of "For He's a Jolly Good Fellow," Alma and a friend peeked into the banquet room to see what the fuss was about. Alma realized the object of the crowd's adulation was the man she had danced with for an entire evening just a week earlier. When Rattenbury and several other banquet goers emerged from the ballroom to have a cigar and nightcap in the lounge, Alma reintroduced herself.

"The memory of that singing had gone to my head," she later wrote, remembering that night, "and though I had resolved, as you know, never to marry again, but to devote myself to my music, that song seemed to make all the difference...Well, my dear, if I don't love him, I simply don't know what love is."

No doubt the circumstances of the banquet suitably impressed Alma, and Ratz likely welcomed the renewed attention of this beautiful woman. He was the man of the hour and this encounter made him feel the stars over his personal life had finally aligned.

When and how the couple consummated their relationship is not known, but by 1924 Alma had moved into a home in James Bay near Beacon Hill Park. She supported herself and Christopher by giving piano lessons and was warmly received by the women in the community. Her home on Niagara Street also became the location for regular discreet meetings with Rattenbury.

As time passed, the couple felt the need for discretion fade. They became ever bolder, meeting in public and even embracing without embarrassment. In the 26 years he had been married to Florrie, Rattenbury had never been as lovesick as he was with this younger woman. To his friends he appeared completely bewitched! Their liaison was so obvious it soon became the subject of delicious whispered gossip in Rattenbury's social circle.

For his part, Ratz believed everyone in Victoria already knew he and Florrie had been enduring an abysmal marriage for years. Confidently, he assumed his friends would understand his extramarital affair. Besides, he had been trying to convince Florrie to give him a divorce for some time and Florrie would hear nothing of it.

Rattenbury's assumption that his friends would condone his affair with Alma was wrong. He was 56 when he met Alma, and Victoria's rich and powerful found the relationship deplorable. They urged Rattenbury to set things right, and he laboured to follow their advice.

Again he tried to get Florrie to consent to divorce — and again he met with denial. Then he adopted another course of action that would eventually cause him to be ostracized by even his closest friends.

Rattenbury ordered a moving company to arrive at his Oak Bay home unannounced and directed it to clear the house of all furniture. As the movers carried furniture out the front door, Florrie and her Chinese servant, Wee, returned the most valuable pieces through the back. She moved them into the one room in the house for which she had the only key and refused to give them up.

Ratz was furious. He responded by having the electricity turned off in the house.

Quickly, though, he realized the community was not on his side. Food hampers began to arrive for Florrie. The women of Oak Bay saw what was happening and decided it was unfair. Though Florrie had rarely spoken to any of them, they judged her to be a victim and provided support. When she successfully gained a court injunction declaring she had a right to live in the house, Ratz gave up his campaign of harassment.

Instead, he took a two-month holiday with Alma, reputedly a cruise in the Mediterranean, and concocted a new plan to force Florrie's surrender.

Much to his wife's dismay, on his return he brought Alma to the Oak Bay home and entertained her there. On one occasion they were making such a spectacle of themselves, loudly singing duets as Alma played the piano, that Mary was forced to complain on her mother's behalf. Alma's presence in the house was causing her mother a dangerous level of stress, she said, and Mary feared for Florrie's health.

Mary did not anticipate Alma's heartless response. The young woman began pounding out a rendition of the funeral march so loudly that no one in the house could escape the chords.

Rattenbury's ploy worked.

At Mary and Frank's urging, Florrie resignedly began divorce proceedings. She and Ratz were finally granted freedom from each other on January 28, 1925. In settlement, Rattenbury was required to pay Florrie alimony of $225 a month, and he had to build her a new home in a location of her choosing.

Florrie saw a chance to fire one last salvo in the bitter divorce and selected a lot at the top of Prospect Place, just off Oak Bay Avenue, for her new home. There, in full sight of Iechinihl, she planned to be a nagging reminder until her death.

Alma also finalized her divorce, and on April 8, 1925, the couple were married in Bellingham, Washington. Though they removed the social stigma of their affair, they were never readmitted to the city's cultural community. Alma's recital engagements vanished. Ratz was also shunned. Friends avoided him on the street and ignored him at his club. People who might have been gracious to the famous architect before the divorce, displayed their real feelings and found it easy to give him a cold shoulder socially and professionally.

The Meddling Madonna

Rattenbury was too much in love to care. On June 2, 1925, he wrote to his sister Kate to tell her he was married. He said that Alma looked "like a fragile Madonna" and that she was "full of sympathy and keen to see the nice side of everyone and flares up with rage over any meanness. Talented in literature and poetry and gets a world of amusement out of any living thing, from bugs upwards; butterflies eat out of her hands."

However, even when the couple had a son, John, two days after Christmas in 1928, the hearts of the community did not soften. Florrie's death on October 13, 1929, sealed off the couple's chance of reacceptance into the tightly knit upper-crust community. Many still saw Florrie, a woman who they believed had devoted her life to cantankerous Rattenbury, as a sad victim.

Alma called on Mary to offer condolences after Florrie's death, and Ratz's daughter harshly rebuffed her. Perhaps Alma truly meant to offer support, but it is more likely she felt the public display of sympathy would show she and Ratz had been forgiven by the children. Regardless, the insensitive act was further proof of Alma's inability to understand how her actions affected others.

An attempt to sue the government for compensation had failed and Rattenbury finally had to liquidate Rattenbury Lands. When that happened, Ratz said he'd had enough. In response to his daughter's rejection, Rattenbury announced he, Alma, Christopher, and baby John would leave the country forever. He changed his will, disinheriting both Mary and Frank. Instead he left his entire estate to Alma and her two children. Possibly as a further slight to Mary and Frank for not welcoming Alma into their lives, Rattenbury arranged to give his Chinese manservant, Foy, an allowance that would continue for the rest of his life.

Then Ratz started packing.

In spite of all his achievements, when Rattenbury waved farewell, his son Frank was the only person in Victoria who waved back.

Chapter 9

Chauffeur and Lover

I n June 1903, Rattenbury wrote to his mother from the CPR hotel he had recently enlarged in Field to report with some pride that a book he had been given showed the Rattenburys could claim a proud history in Okehampton, Devonshire.

"Rattenburys seem to have played a great part in it in the days of Henry VIII and Charles I," he wrote. "They were Mayors often, and entertained at their house Charles I on two occasions."

With his decision to leave Canada irrevocable, Ratz intended to have John christened in the parish church his family had so generously supported in Okehampton. Perhaps he also thought he might recapture there some of the status and pride he had lost in Victoria.

Their journey to England took six months. With a nursemaid for John, the Rattenburys sailed through the Panama Canal and on to Havana. They also went to New York and by train to Montreal, where they boarded another ship for Europe. After a tour of the Mediterranean and northern France, they finally reached England in the summer of 1930. Ratz was disappointed to find that far from being a thriving place cloaked in proud Rattenbury family memories, Okehampton was "an ugly, dirty and stupid town." He and Alma stayed there only a short time before moving to Bournemouth.

In Bournemouth the couple could almost feel as if they had never left Canada. In many ways the city reminded them of Victoria. It was on the seaside and had become a popular place for the retired and well-to-do.

They rented a tidy cottage at 5 Manor Road named Villa Madeira, a few minutes' stroll from cliffs that overlooked the ocean. Rattenbury had no architectural work to speak of, but he soon occupied himself in other ways. With a friend he developed and produced antiseptic products and mouthwash, for instance, and he helped promote Alma's reinvigorated musical career.

Chauffeur and Lover

Once her grand piano arrived from Canada, she began to write popular songs. With tunes and lyrics in hand, Ratz managed to get her an audition with the largest music publisher in London. Van Leir, the head of Keith Prowse and Co., was enthralled and he promptly agreed to publish one of her songs. Alma's career blossomed, and when her tunes were recorded, she enjoyed some minor success. She produced several records with tenor Frank Titterton, and her musical talents were celebrated in special broadcast performances on the BBC.

Bournemouth became party central for a new group of friends attracted by Alma's celebrity status, and the couple happily entertained long into the summer evenings, to the dismay of their neighbours. Although Rattenbury's finances continued to shrink amid the financial collapses of the Depression, they lived a comfortable life.

Though she probably would have rather settled in London, closer to the theatre and music world, Alma found a niche in the community just the same. Outwardly the couple appeared to be wealthy, due in large part to Alma's extravagance. She was known to be overly generous, often giving away money and possessions as if doing so had no impact on the household finances. She gaily enjoyed all the attention, but life in their Bournemouth cottage was far from perfect.

By 1930, Rattenbury was showing his 60-plus years. He had begun to lose his hearing, and his features offered evidence that his drinking was becoming heavy. As well, the relationship, charged with sexual energy in the beginning, had become decidedly less active. Alma later revealed the two stopped sleeping together after John was born. Rattenbury's age and his heavy drinking may have been a root cause.

It did not seem to alter their genuine affection for each other, however. Alma accepted Ratz's loss of physical interest in her matter-of-factly. She used her best humour to pull him out of what became a constant depression. She drank with him and saw to his needs domestically.

Rattenbury existed in a state of gloom most of the time, brooding about his past and his anemic finances. While his skills as an architect had pulled him from the brink of financial disaster two times before, now all he could hope for was the occasional design job on speculation. Even those were few and far between.

Money was a real worry for him. There was the cost of their rented accommodation, the charges to keep Christopher in boarding school in nearby Southborne, and the burden of servicing Alma's expensive tastes. Rattenbury cast about, trying to find a means to replenish his bank account. He tried to convert his Oak Bay home into an inn, but the residents of Victoria had not forgotten the scandal and hardly wanted a reminder in the form of a commercial establishment smack dab in the middle of their residential neighbourhood. How he managed to maintain his lifestyle on what he had was a mystery.

Alma, on the other hand, was generally happy leading a celibate life with Rattenbury at Villa Madeira. As well as friends in Bournemouth and London, Alma had grown close to her maid, Irene Riggs. The daughter of the local gravedigger, Irene was a decade younger than Alma, but the two got on more as friends than as mistress and servant. They ventured into Bournemouth for shopping on a regular basis and often spent quiet "girl time" together.

Just as often, however, the evenings they shared were strikingly out of the ordinary. With John safely tucked into bed and Ratz passed out in his room, Alma would sometimes launch into a frantic bout of rambling or housecleaning. Often these flurries of activity occurred when Alma had consumed more than her normal ration of dinner cocktails. With a burst of unexplained energy, she would wander about the house, wringing her hands, talking constantly, and drinking to excess. When she finally ran out of energy, Irene put her to bed. Alma's behaviour was later considered suspicious, and there was speculation that it was a symptom of possible cocaine abuse.

On these occasions she became decidedly aggressive, and her normal soothing manner towards her husband could vanish in a flood of angry words. As the years passed, Rattenbury's conversations with Alma slipped more and more often to the subject of suicide. Prospects of a less secure future bedeviled him, and he judged his life to have reached a dead-end.

On one night in July 1934, his drunken suicide threats coincided with one of Alma's own frenetic episodes. Rather than coaxing him to smile, she lashed out. "Why don't you do it then?" Alma angrily taunted.

Rattenbury, fuelled by alcohol, reacted with an attack, leaving Alma with a black eye. Then he charged from Villa Madeira, headed towards the oceanside cliffs with her dare on his mind. Sometime later he reappeared, sober and sorry, and Alma forgave him. She handled Ratz more gently in future.

In September 1934, the couple decided to hire a chauffeur. Considering Rattenbury's fixation about money, it must have been Alma's doing.

George Percy Stoner, a short, stocky young boy, who lived with his grandmother about five kilometres from Bournemouth, was the son of a bricklayer. His childhood was an unstable one as his father had moved from town to town to take on temporary jobs. Stoner's schooling suffered, and he was described as not seeming to be "very brilliant in mind." He had slim experience, especially working in the well-to-do surroundings of Bournemouth, but the Rattenburys hired him anyway.

His duties in their employ included driving John to and from prep school or taking Alma and Irene on shopping excursions. When he wasn't driving, he did odd jobs about the house and then returned to his grandmother's home in Ensbury Park for the night.

It took only a month before he moved into a spare bedroom at the Villa Madeira. Apparently Alma found other things for the boy to do. Still sexually vital, she seduced him. By November, she had convinced herself she was in love with him.

Stoner quickly became a fixture in the place and appeared to have a cordial relationship with Rattenbury, often chatting or playing cards with him in the evenings.

However, as Christmas 1934 approached, Stoner evidently decided he had fallen in love with Alma. Inexperienced in matters of the heart, he became preoccupied with her and found it difficult to separate his roles of houseboy and bedmate. With youthful bravado he tried to impress Alma, as young men so often do when smitten and afraid the object of their affection might lose interest. He invented a life of mystery for himself and took to carrying a dagger. He also showed signs of jealousy whenever Alma bestowed small affections on Ratz.

Alma seemed to enjoy the charade, but by the beginning of 1935 she began to have qualms. When she suggested to Stoner that they should consider ending their affair, he reacted violently and even threatened her life. Alma brushed off the threat as theatrics and tried to smooth the waters between them.

About six months after Stoner joined the household, Alma found herself overdrawn at the bank. This was a regular occurrence three or four times a year, and as she had done before, Alma dreamed up an excuse to get Rattenbury to part with more of his money.

She suffered a smouldering form of tuberculosis, and in March 1935 she used that as her reason. She needed an operation in London, she told Rattenbury, and it would cost £250.

Ratz, as always, came through. With her bankroll, she and Stoner left Bournemouth for London on Wednesday, March 20. Without conscience, they registered at the posh Royal Palace Hotel in Kensington as brother and sister. They were given separate bedrooms, but used only one.

During the three days they spent in London, Alma treated Stoner to the high life. She enjoyed herself immensely and was so comfortable she even wrote to her children from the hotel. Stoner happily played the part of husband.

To help him fit the part of a dashing man about town, Alma took Stoner to Harrod's. With her "operation money" she proceeded on a shopping spree that did not end until Stoner was the owner of a new wardrobe. In just one afternoon, Alma's generosity lavished purchases of more than £40 on Stoner. It was a sum he couldn't have earned in his houseboy position even after nine months of work.

The time they shared was delightful, but Alma recognized it as only a game of make-believe and expected Stoner to do the same. When they got back to Villa Madeira on Friday night, however, Stoner seemed incapable of separating his reality from the London fantasy.

That Sunday, Ratz sank into one of his morbid depressions. He was having difficulty arranging the financing to build an apartment block he had designed and was wallowing in his frustration. Alma decided to take tea in her bedroom with him, hoping to entice a better mood.

As it was Irene's half-day off, Stoner was pressed into service to make their tea.

In the solitude of Alma's bedroom, Ratz talked

about his feelings and described the detail of a book he had been reading while she was away. The novel concerned a middle-aged character who, on the verge of suicide, meets a young woman. Ratz told Alma how much he identified with the main character and even read her a particularly poignant passage he had marked. The character was explaining why the relationship had to end.

"...a woman, let's put it, always wants more than a man. And when a man's a good deal older, she wants a good deal more than him. A good deal more than he can give her. It takes all his time for a young man to keep pace with a young girl. And an old man hasn't a chance of doing it. And then — she usually goes somewhere else to make up the deficiency."

Months earlier, Alma and Ratz had had a discussion not unlike the scene in the novel. At the time, Alma had alluded to her relationship with Stoner and had told her husband she intended to live her own life. She had decided Ratz did not care about her affair, or at least had never shown he actually knew it was happening. He slept in a bedroom a floor beneath hers, was becoming deaf, and consumed much more alcohol than he needed to sleep soundly each night. Still, from what he said now, she wondered if Ratz knew Stoner had become her lover after all.

Chauffeur and Lover

Alma reacted to Ratz sympathetically. The door to her room, normally open, was closed that afternoon.

Whatever happened in privacy worked to tug Ratz from his mood. Later that afternoon, Alma appeared cheerful. She had convinced Ratz to visit a business acquaintance she believed would help Ratz fund his apartment block project. The friend lived in Bridport, about two hours from Bournemouth, in a large manor house. Because of the distance, Alma suggested they should stay overnight at the friend's home. Rattenbury agreed with her and appeared at least a little excited about the scheme.

After tea, Alma got Ratz settled in his drawing room armchair with a stiff drink and a kiss. Then she made a telephone call to their friend to discuss arrangements.

Stoner stood near the telephone with her, fuming. While the couple were upstairs he had heard snippets of their conversation. He suspected the closed bedroom door could mean only one thing. He accused Alma of trying to calm Ratz down by making love to him, just as she had done so often with Stoner himself. He raged with jealousy.

When Alma hung up the telephone, Stoner thrust what she took to be a revolver in front of her face. If they stayed overnight, he said, Alma and her husband would be sharing a bedroom, and Stoner would have none of that. Angrily he vowed to kill her if she went to Bridport with Rattenbury.

Alma told Stoner nothing had happened in the bedroom. Gradually she managed to calm her young lover with whispered promises she would never again close her door while Ratz was in the room. As far as Bridport went, Alma assured him their friend's manor house was large and had plenty of bedrooms. They would sleep alone, she promised.

Apparently calmed, Stoner left Villa Madeira to visit his grandmother. For the next several hours Alma and Ratz played cards. At 9:30 she decided to retire to her room to pack for their journey.

To Alma, all seemed right with the world, but it had never been more wrong.

Chapter 10
A Mallet and
a Murder

I rene returned from her half-day off to a silent Villa Madeira.

After heading to her room and preparing for bed, she felt hungry and decided to get a quick snack in the peaceful quiet of the kitchen. As she made her way past the master's quarters she thought she heard an unusual sound and took a peek. Finding the bedroom empty, she listened again. Perhaps Mr. Rattenbury had taken too much whisky and fallen asleep in his drawing room chair. The noise could have been a snore.

Deciding not to take the chance of awakening him

by moving about in the kitchen, Irene backtracked to her room and finished her bedtime preparations. A few minutes later, while heading to the bathroom, she was startled to see Stoner in his pajamas, leaning on the railing that overlooked the ground floor hall. He told her he was just checking to see if the lights had been turned off.

Irene returned to her room and within moments had a visitor. Alma, in a cheery mood, had come to tell her about the trip that she and Ratz planned for the following day. She also recounted her spat with Stoner in some detail. She said she thought she had straightened things with him, but she wasn't sure if Stoner would be driving them to Bridport or not.

Irene assumed the storm that had occurred while she was away had truly blown over and she could look forward to a quiet few days alone. She settled in and was almost asleep when the sound of someone rushing down the stairs pulled her back. She lay listening, arguing with herself about whether to climb out of her warm bed. She decided not to move.

The mysterious movement in the hallway had been Alma.

After visiting with Irene, Alma returned to her own room and Stoner's arms. For a few minutes, while they whispered and embraced, all seemed normal. But when Alma heard the sound of a heavy groan coming from somewhere below, she broke free. She knew the groan had to be Ratz. It was unusual and frightening. She rushed to the hall and ran down the stairs barefoot, bound for the drawing room where she had left Ratz with his bottle less than an hour before.

Reaching the doorway, she found him slumped forward in his chair. At first she relaxed. Ratz looked as if he had only passed out drunk in an awkward position. When she moved closer, however, she quickly realized something was terribly wrong. Bending down to look at him, she saw that Ratz's right eye was swollen and marked by an ugly purple bruise. His gray hair was matted and wet. She looked about him and saw blood. It was on his chair and pooled near his feet on the carpet.

Her first conclusion was that he had fallen and hurt himself. Resignedly, she knew he would have to be roused. Once he was awake she could tend to the cut and put him to bed.

Instead of reaching for him, though, Alma grabbed for his unfinished whisky and gulped. Her heart was still pumping wildly because of the scare the groan had given her. She thought the bracing liquor would settle her nerves. Instead of helping, the harsh taste made her retch. She drank again and this time managed to swallow a second mouthful while she stared at her husband.

Moving to get a better look at his face, Alma

stepped on Rattenbury's false teeth, evidently knocked from his mouth when he fell. She picked them up. Having his teeth in would make it easier for him to speak. But when she tried to lift his head and reinsert them, she realized Ratz was far more badly hurt than she had thought. The full impact of his condition suddenly dawned on her and she screamed to Irene for help.

Shouting an order to call for a doctor, she also told her maid to get Stoner. After he appeared in his pajamas, the three of them managed to lift Ratz from the armchair and carry him to his bed. While Stoner went to pick up the doctor, Irene nervously undressed Ratz. Alma was no help at all. She had poured herself another drink and only stood by the bed, wondering out loud what could have happened.

When their family physician, Dr. O'Donnell, arrived he quickly assessed the circumstances. Ratz's head was covered in blood. His breathing was laboured and his heart was beating slowly. The doctor knew he would need the help of the local surgeon and telephoned for him immediately. In the interim he could attend to Alma.

She appeared intoxicated and overwrought, nervously pacing in the drawing room. O'Donnell, who also thought that Ratz must have fallen and hit his head, asked her if she knew what had happened.

Alma replied with a hysterical statement of the obvious. "Look at all the blood," she screamed. "He must have been attacked!" Then another thought occurred to her. She told the doctor Rattenbury had been reading a novel about suicide. Alma retrieved it from the piano and pushed it into the doctor's hands. She urged him to read it himself and see.

When the surgeon arrived, he found Alma clumsily trying to minister to her husband while the doctor looked on. To the surgeon, it was obvious Ratz had to be moved to a hospital where his injuries could be properly examined. He summoned an ambulance. At the Strathallen Nursing Home, the surgeon concluded Rattenbury had been hit on the head three times with a blunt instrument of some kind.

At 2:00 a.m., the Bournemouth police appeared at Villa Madeira in the form of Constable Bagwell and, shortly later, Inspector Mills. Based on the surgeon's findings, they told the household, an investigation would have to be made. Bagwell questioned Alma and got a rather undescriptive rundown of the sequence of events. In her statement she claimed a yell had brought her running to the drawing room.

Mills observed Alma was extremely agitated and appeared to be intoxicated, but he questioned her as well. Repeating what she had told Bagwell, Alma corrected her statement slightly. It was a groan that had first got her attention, she said.

The inspector asked if the French doors that opened to the garden off the drawing room had been closed when she rushed to her husband.

Alma told him yes. In fact, she added, they had been locked. In a sudden moment of sobriety, however, Alma realized that if the doors were locked, the police would suspect the attacker was one of the people living in the house. Because of their affair, Stoner would be an immediate suspect. She returned to the whisky and drank more while the police searched for clues. When Mills left to go to the nursing home, Alma cornered Bagwell.

Bagwell later testified that she said, "I know who done it. I did it with a mallet."

Bagwell asked her why.

"Ratz has lived too long," she said.

The constable asked her to show him the mallet.

"It is hidden," Alma slurred. Then, just as quickly realizing she might be confessing to murder, she recanted and blamed Stoner.

Bagwell did not know which of the drunken statements he should believe. Alma seemed to be riding an intoxicated pendulum of indecision, one minute confessing and the next denying that confession and pointing the finger of blame elsewhere.

In a whisky-induced fog, she was now also desperately trying to get Bagwell to forget what she said. She offered him a bribe of £10, and when he refused it, she began pursuing him about the house, suggesting other ways he might be convinced to forget her confession. She tried to kiss him. The constable found it impossible to evade Alma's advances and decided to wait for Inspector Mills' return out in the garden. Alma would have followed him there to press her offer more aggressively had Irene not physically prevented it by forcing her mistress into a chair and sitting on her.

At 3:30 a.m., Mills reappeared. He told Alma that Ratz was in grave condition and he cautioned her to be careful about what she said. Any statements would be noted in the investigation record and employed as evidence in a trial that was certain to happen.

Alma, now practically in shock, began a rambling statement for Mills in which she took full blame.

"He gave me the book. He has lived too long. He said, 'Dear, dear.' I will tell you in the morning where the mallet is. Have you told the Coroner yet? I shall make a better job of it next time. Irene does not know. I made a proper muddle of it. I thought I was strong enough."

A few minutes later, Dr. O'Donnell also returned to

Villa Madeira. Stoner, who had been waiting patiently in the car at the nursing home, was with him. Several more policemen had been called to the scene, and Alma was staggering about, clinging to one policeman after another. The home was a madhouse. Every light was on, and Alma had put a phonograph recording of one of her songs on a record player at full volume. She was excitedly trying to talk over the din.

O'Donnell guided Alma to her room and administered a half grain of morphia in an attempt to calm her down. It seemed to work, but the moment of peace was quickly replaced by a bout of frenzy when Alma concocted another possible suspect. She rushed from her room and accosted Mills with her new solution to the mystery.

"I know who did it — his son," she told him.

Mills, thinking she meant six-year-old John, who was fast asleep in Alma's room in spite of all the noise, asked her his age.

Alma replied immediately that he was 32, meaning she was referring to Frank. "But he is not here," she said, suddenly realizing her idea was impossible.

Mills and O'Donnell returned Alma, now barely able to walk, to her room and put her into bed.

She remained in a drug-aided stupor until 6:00 a.m.

In the meantime, another policeman had arrived at

A Mallet and a Murder

Villa Madeira. While Detective Inspector Carter waited for Alma to awaken and dress, he questioned Stoner.

Stoner said he had gone to bed at 8:00 p.m. the night before and was awakened at 10:30 p.m. by Alma's screams. He claimed he had asked Alma what happened and that she told him she didn't know. He also told Carter he had not heard the couple quarrelling.

The detective inspector was apparently satisfied by Stoner's calmly delivered statement. At 8:00 a.m. he returned to Alma and charged her with the wounding of her husband.

Again, Alma made a statement, but this time she too was calm and sensible. "At about 9 p.m. I was playing cards with my husband when he dared me to kill him as he wanted to die. I picked up the mallet. He then said, 'You have not guts enough to do it.' I then hit him with the mallet. I hid the mallet outside the house. I would have shot him if I had a gun."

Alma signed the statement Carter had recorded and then, without fuss, was taken to the Bournemouth Police Station. To be sure no mistake had been made, he again charged her with the wounding.

"That is right," she said. "I did it deliberately and would do it again."

In the days that followed, the police search for the mallet Alma claimed to have hidden in the garden turned up nothing. Either unable or unwilling to disclose its location, Alma offered little help. They continued their hunt, however, confident it would eventually be found and her confession proved.

At Villa Madeira, Irene and Stoner did their jobs without employers to serve. During a trip in the Rattenburys' car a few days after the arrest, Stoner drove Irene past his grandmother's home. That was where he had borrowed the mallet, he told her, bragging without guilt about how he had used gloves to avoid leaving fingerprints.

Irene believed him. She had no doubt her mistress was incapable of the attack on Rattenbury. That left only Stoner to blame — and left Irene with a dilemma.

To that point the illicit affair between her mistress and the chauffeur was still a secret of the household. Irene knew that if she told the police, all of Bournemouth would quickly learn of Alma's shameless adultery. Though she was not Catholic, the next day she took her usual evening off to visit a local priest. She needed guidance in this delicate matter of the heart.

When she got back to Villa Madeira, she found her mother waiting with a warning. Stoner had apparently gotten so drunk that a taxi had to bring him home. He had been calling around Bournemouth, trying to find Irene.

A Mallet and a Murder

When she approached him, she found Stoner in a strange state. He told Irene he was going to go to London to see Alma and turn himself in. Apparently a letter Alma sent from Holloway Prison, pitifully asking him to visit with news about Rattenbury's condition, had convinced him to come clean.

The next morning, while Stoner rode the train to London, word reached Irene that her master had died. She immediately called the police and told them Stoner's story about the mallet. As Stoner stepped off the train in London, Detective Inspector Carter was waiting to charge him with Rattenbury's murder.

Chapter 11
Trial of the Century

he day after Rattenbury died, Stoner stated his guilt to a detective constable while waiting for his appearance in court.

"When I did the job," he told Detective Constable Gates, "I believed he was asleep. I hit him and then came upstairs and told Mrs. Rattenbury. She rushed down then. You see, I watched through the French windows and saw her kiss him goodnight, then leave the room. I waited and crept in through the French window, which was unlocked. I think he must have been asleep when I hit him..."

Stoner maintained complete certainty that Alma was in love with him. He asked the police to be sure and have a doctor with her when she was told of his arrest "because she will go out of her mind."

She may have been in love, but Stoner's act had definitely taken a toll on her feelings. In a letter written to Irene from Holloway Prison on April 18, she made it clear she held Stoner accountable for the terrible mess that her life and her children's had become.

"Two times have found my feelings very hard and bitter — Oh, my God, appallingly so — but have managed to drown these feelings and get one's heart soft again," she wrote.

It was late May before the trial was held at London's Old Bailey law courts, where the lovers would face a judge and jury.

Stoner had made the case against himself straightforward with his simple, matter-of-fact confession. The Crown's case against Alma was less clear. Her confessions the night of the attack had been confused and contradictory. It was obvious she was intoxicated and later drugged with the full knowledge of her police inquisitors. Besides, Alma had only admitted to wounding Ratz. Stoner, on the other hand, confessed to murder.

In England, the trial was a sensation. Long lines of

spectators gathered on the sidewalk outside the court for hours before it was to open. Some even sold their place in line to others who were so curious they were willing to pay for a chair in the gallery.

Alma must have been a beguiling beauty in the grim surroundings of the Old Bailey. She looked dignified in a navy blue dress made of silk with a fur cape clipped over her shoulders.

On the third day of the trial she was called to the stand to testify in her defense.

Alma had pleaded not guilty to all charges, blaming her confessions on hysteria and confusion created by drugs. Stoner also pleaded not guilty, blaming an addiction to cocaine as the root cause for his violent act.

Alma answered her lawyer's questions in a composed, clear voice, and together they recounted her history for the court. She told the court she had been married twice before Rattenbury and had been his wife for seven or eight years. Of her two children, only John was Rattenbury's.

Her lawyer, T. J. O'Connor, tried to establish a picture of a lonely woman in a marriage that was cold and loveless.

He asked if she and Rattenbury had lived together as man and wife after the birth of their son and she said no.

"On what terms were you with your husband?" O'Connor asked.

"Quite friendly."

"No marital intimacy, but you were friendly?"

"Absolutely."

When he asked her if her married life had been a happy one, Alma rocked her hand in the air.

He asked if they quarrelled often.

"Not very frequent," she replied.

"Were they severe when they occurred, or were they just trifling quarrels?"

"It all depended on whether Mr. Rattenbury got into a temper or not. Sometimes he did."

O'Connor carefully led Alma through an account of the night in July when Ratz had struck her and blackened her eye.

That night "he was queer morbid," she told the court, "and there was the usual talk of committing suicide, so I asked him, seeing that he was always frightening me that he was going to commit suicide, why he did not do it for a change?"

O'Connor had set up his picture of a wife devoted to her husband and children despite a history of assault. He also needed to dispel the image, produced earlier by the prosecution, of a woman who had lied to get money so she could finance an "orgy" in London.

"What were the relations between you and your husband as regards money? Was he free with money?"

"Very close — well, not very generous," she replied, admitting she lied to Ratz to get money all through her married life.

The tawdry affair that the spectators had come to hear about was undressed next. Alma admitted to seducing young Stoner two months after he was hired as the Rattenbury chauffeur. She said they regularly had sexual relations after that.

"What attitude did your husband take towards this, if he knew it?"

"None whatsoever."

"Did he know of it?"

"He must have known because he told me to live my own life quite a few years ago."

O'Connor then walked her through the events of the Sunday leading up to the murder. Alma told of Stoner's jealousy and suspicions and recounted how, after overhearing her conversation with Ratz about the trip to Bridport, he had threatened to kill her.

"He was very annoyed at my going to Bridport. We had quite an unpleasant time about it, but afterwards I thought it was all right." She explained that Stoner had thought she and Rattenbury would have to share a bedroom and that she told him they would not.

Alma described how she had played cards with her husband and then gone to her room to pack. Sometime after 10:00 p.m. she had heard Irene arrive and went to tell her about the trip. Then she said she returned to her bedroom and waited for Stoner. He arrived a while later in his pajamas. He seemed "queer" to her.

Stoner told her he was in trouble but refused to tell her why.

"I thought he was in trouble outside, you know — his mother or like that — and then I said I was strong enough to bear anything and he told me that I was not going to Bridport the next day as he had hurt Ratz. It did not penetrate my head what he did say to me at all until I heard Ratz groan, and then my brain became alive and I jumped out of bed."

Alma told the court that Stoner had confessed to hitting Rattenbury with a mallet, which he had then hidden outside the house.

She said she found Ratz in his armchair. "I tried to rub his hands; they were cold. I tried to take his pulse and I shook him to try and make him speak." Stepping on his false teeth made her scream, she said. "I cannot remember, only vaguely. I took a drink of whisky to stop myself being sick."

Pressed by her lawyer, she said she then poured more whisky and drank it.

"I tried to become insensible, to block out the picture."

O'Connor asked her if she had murdered her husband or known what Stoner had planned to do.

"I would have prevented it if I had known half — a quarter of a minute before, naturally," she replied.

Stoner's lawyer, J. D. Casswell, then took over questioning Alma. He wanted to prove Alma had seduced his client and asked if she had suggested they live together in Rattenbury's house. Alma said the decision had been a mutual one.

"Did you think it might have had a deleterious effect on him?"

Alma replied indignantly. "No, I would never have started it if I had."

And what about her relationship with Rattenbury? Had she told Stoner that she and her husband no longer slept together as a way of enticing the boy to her bed? She said she had not.

Casswell moved to the subject of drugs and asked her if she had ever taken them.

"No, absolutely not," Alma said.

"Are you quite sure of that?"

"Absolutely."

"From time to time we have heard that you used to get very excited at times and then get drowsy afterwards?" Stoner's counsel was intimating to the jury this may have been a sign of drug use, but Alma countered with another reason.

"Well all my life with Mr. Rattenbury was so what we call monotonous that at times I used to take too many cocktails to liven up one's spirits — take them to excess, say, or wine." She told Casswell that Stoner was upset with her drinking as he didn't drink much himself, and she stopped doing it to excess after he arrived.

Her answers were not what the lawyer wanted the jury members to hear. He wanted them to view Alma as a bad influence on the young man, so he changed his tactics. He asked Alma about Stoner's claim that he was addicted to drugs.

Alma said that once, when Stoner claimed he needed to go to London to get drugs for himself, she had talked to her doctor about the problem. She said the doctor had told her he could help Stoner with his addiction.

"Now had you any doubt that that boy at that time had such a craving that he went to London and nothing you said would stop him?" Casswell asked.

Alma surprised him with her answer. "To be perfectly candid, I was not certain then, and I am not certain now."

Though Alma had admitted to drinking too much

and beginning a sexual relationship with a boy young enough to be her son, her testimony so far had clearly damaged the Crown's case against her. All her answers were given clearly in a low, rich voice, and her composure as well as her attire seemed to have impressed the jury.

Now it was the prosecution's turn at Alma, and R. P. Croom-Johnson was determined to show her in a different light. He questioned her about Rattenbury's finances.

Alma told him she understood Ratz to be well-off and admitted to deceiving her husband to get more of his money. But when Croom-Johnson tried to show she was conniving about it, her answers proved she did not have a head for figures. She had no real understanding of the state of Rattenbury's declining fortunes. The money, as she had pointed out, was to balance the household budget, and the jury seemed to believe her.

Croom-Johnson decided to play the seduction card instead.

"You have told us that on Sunday night Stoner came into your bedroom and got into bed with you?"

"Yes," Alma replied.

"Was that something that happened frequently?"

"Oh, always."

"Always? Were you fond of your little boy John?"

Croom-Johnson asked.

"I love both my children."

"Were you fond of John?"

"Naturally."

"Did John sleep in the same room?"

"Yes," Alma answered, "but little John was always asleep."

In his follow-up question, Croom-Johnson indicated he thought Alma was admitting to an incredible lack of judgment.

"I did not consider that was dreadful," Alma argued. "I did not consider it an intrigue with Stoner," because John was a sound sleeper.

Once again, the prosecution's line of questioning led Croom-Johnson to a dead-end. John obviously was a sound sleeper. He had remained asleep throughout the ruckus on the night of the murder, so Alma's contention seemed credible.

Croom-Johnson decided to attack her memory of the night of the murder, with questions that implied she could not possibly have forgotten so much of the evening.

Alma said she remembered putting a towel on Rattenbury's head, rubbing his hands, trying to replace his false teeth, and nothing more.

"Do you recollect Dr. O'Donnell coming?"

"I cannot," Alma replied. She was being selective about what she recalled, because on March 28 she had said she remembered Dr. O'Donnell and the surgeon arriving, as well as Dr. O'Donnell coming back and giving her morphia. But Alma managed to be consistent in her answers to the prosecution's barrage. When she was shown Detective Inspector Carter's notes and her signed statement from the morning after the murder, Alma said she couldn't remember it either.

Previous police witnesses had confirmed she was drinking the night of the murder, but the seasoned investigators did not think her condition made her unfit to make statements. Carter said she was lucid the morning after and had signed his notes to confirm they were correct. At the police station she had admitted it again. If she had not attacked Ratz, why had she confessed?

O'Connor may have worried that the jury was concluding Alma made the confessions because she was a party to the act in some way. He offered the real reason. She had confessed to protect Stoner.

For Stoner's lawyer, the drug defence was a no-win situation. Expert medical opinion disagreed about whether Stoner was a cocaine addict, and there was some doubt as to whether he had ever in fact taken cocaine at all. The young man described the drug he had used as brownish with darker flecks. The doctors called to the witness box told the jury that cocaine, even of the poorest quality, was always pure white. Besides, Stoner earned a paltry £4 a month. The jury must have wondered how he could afford to maintain an expensive cocaine habit on that kind of income.

It did not take long for the jury to deliberate. After just 47 minutes they returned to the court and declared Alma not guilty of murder. She showed no outward signs of relief.

When asked about Stoner's fate, however, they gave the opposite decision. He was declared guilty, but the jury recommended leniency.

Alma reacted physically to the news, appearing to almost collapse. She needed the strong arms of a wardress to be helped from the dock and escorted out of the courtroom.

Stoner stood in the centre of the dock, stoic and alone, while the judge delivered his death sentence.

Chapter 12
Death on the Avon

Alma left the Old Bailey by way of the barrister's entrance to avoid the crowd of press and spectators waiting to catch a glimpse of her leaving. She was taken to a nursing home in Cleveland Gardens, Bayswater. She continued to be in a ragged, fragile state of mind.

Even the next day, when Irene paid a visit, bringing a gift of pink roses, Alma seemed on the verge of a breakdown. Irene, who had been as close to Alma as any friend, listened while Alma talked about committing suicide. She even began the process of planning her funeral with Irene, telling the maid she wanted to be buried in a pink coffin wearing a pink nightgown.

Alma, of course, did not appreciate how much duress her conversation was causing Irene. The nursing home matron finally had to call off the teary meeting in order to relieve poor Irene.

Alone, with few other visitors, Alma was observed reading the newspaper stories about the trial. She could not get Stoner out of her mind and relived, over and over again, the testimony she had given against him. She wrote to him, but a day later determined that only a visit would be appropriate. She pleaded with the nursing home doctor and matron to help her see Stoner.

"If I had just one word with him, even if I just had one look at his face again, he would understand. I must see him once again...can't something be done?"

The doctor tried to help. He petitioned the governor of the prison for permission, but a reply came too late for Alma.

On Monday, June 3, Alma was pampered with a beauty treatment, and the uplifting effects of those few hours seemed to do wonders for her outlook. She wrote to her Bournemouth solicitor that afternoon, instructing him to spare no effort or expense to get an appeal or reprieve for her young lover. Alma seemed confident that newspaper coverage of the trial would increase the popularity of her songs and that money would therefore not be a problem.

When the nursing home doctor paid a visit to Alma in the late afternoon, he too concluded that her attitude had taken a positive shift. Gone was her nervous, hysterical conversation. She seemed calm and controlled and did not object to the suggestion that she remain a patient in the nursing home for at least another month to be sure she was recovered. In fact, Alma seemed anxious to regain her health. She told the doctor of her plans for the future, and he left with hopes for her full recovery.

It is no surprise, then, that he was shocked that evening when the nursing home called to say Alma had discharged herself. He was sure that something had happened in the brief period since his visit to change her mind and her positive attitude.

After he left, Alma wrote a note that described the turn her thoughts and feelings had taken. "If only I thought it would help Stoner I would stay on, but it has been pointed out to me all too vividly that I cannot help him."

After the doctor's visit, Alma was occupied with another. An unidentified friend appeared at the nursing home, and she engaged Alma in serious conversation for several hours. Shortly after 9:30 p.m., the friend informed the matron that Alma had decided to leave and nothing was going to stop her. The friend assured the matron that she was going to arrange for a nurse to be with Alma at all times. When the matron questioned her about where Alma might be going, the friend was vague.

Alma left with her friend in a private car. Strangely, however, only a few hours later she arrived at a different health care facility, the Elizabeth Fullcher nursing home, alone.

She spent the night there, and in the early afternoon borrowed money from one of the nurses. She told the nurse she planned to go out for a while, but would return that evening. The nurse had no way of knowing she was not telling the truth. Instead, Alma took the train to Christchurch and the banks of the River Avon.

After Alma's body was recovered from the river, an autopsy was performed and the results presented at a coroner's inquest in Christchurch. The autopsy showed that Alma had stabbed herself six times. Mentioning the notes found on the riverbank, the coroner concluded Alma had not been of sound mind and had indeed killed herself.

Hours before her funeral, a large crowd gathered at Wimbourne Road cemetery. Alma was to be buried a few metres from Rattenbury's unmarked grave, and the gawkers wanted to be part of this ending to the sordid affair of Villa Madeira.

By the time her coffin arrived at the cemetery, the funeral party was estimated to number more than 3000. They jostled for position and blocked access to the chapel in their eager fight to gain a seat inside. It was an uncontrolled sideshow, but the large gathering did produce an advantage for Stoner.

Circulating in the crowd was a man gathering signatures on a petition to reprieve Alma's young lover. A campaign for a reprieve had begun just a few hours after the death sentence was pronounced. A small committee, headed by a Bournemouth accountant named F. W. Thisleton, wanted to see Stoner's sentence commuted to life imprisonment, which could lead, in time, to Stoner's release.

Their appeal in the petition was based on nine points. Most centred on Stoner's age and the belief that he had been led astray and was a victim of drugs and misplaced passion.

The committee prepared and circulated petition forms with enough space to record 144,000 signatures, and the press had a field day, continuing to print lurid reports of the case for weeks.

The nation went wild. Volunteers from all walks of life were drawn to the effort to save young Stoner. As the date of his appeal loomed, nearly 350,000 signatures had been gathered.

Rattenbury's murder had, like Rattenbury's life, become surrounded by controversy.

Crowds with placards calling for mercy circulated on the street outside the Court of Criminal Appeal in London as Stoner took his place at the dock.

Casswell, the lawyer who had defended Stoner in the murder trial, handled the appeal. He recounted the trial evidence in voluminous detail, so specific and redundantly reviewed that the judges were forced to interrupt him.

Casswell's appeal was based on the fact that the couple had been tried together. Stoner, his lawyer told the judges, had been unwilling to testify out of concern that his testimony might implicate Alma. Stoner had no idea Alma would do precisely that to him.

The lawyer argued that if Alma had been tried first, Stoner would have been free to tell his side of the story without worry for Alma's case.

Like Stoner's original defence, it was a weak argument. The judges conferred before pronouncing their judgment on the appeal.

The Chief Justice called the whole case squalid and sordid. "The fact, if it be a fact, that a lad of good character was corrupted by an abandoned woman old enough to be his mother raises no question of law that can be employed as a ground of appeal," he said.

The case was dismissed.

Stoner's only hope lay in the hands of the Home Secretary, who had to deal, reluctantly, with the political mess created by the petition. Should he just abide by the court's decision or intervene to pacify the enormous tide of public opinion to the contrary?

The Home Secretary opted for political safety.

On June 25 he commuted Stoner's death sentence to life in prison. Stoner served seven years in prison. In 1942, only 26 years old, he was released as a model prisoner and even allowed to join the army. He survived World War II, married, and spent the rest of his life in obscurity.

Epilogue

Though in his final years Francis Mawson Rattenbury was a bitter man filled with self-recrimination about a life wasted, his legacy to the people of British Columbia is glorious. The impact he had on the development of the province was profound and lasting.

During his career he designed and built some of the most beautiful government buildings in the country. His record of achievements stands as a reminder of his creativity and genius. The BC Legislative Buildings, the Vancouver Court House (now the Vancouver Art Gallery), and the splendid Lady of Victoria Harbour — the Empress Hotel — are solid evidence he left the mark he so desperately wanted to place on history.

His buildings are landmarks by which visitors remember the province as surely as they remember its mountain scenery. The formal requirements he espoused for planning green space that the public could enjoy, and his opinion that development should be monitored and carefully planned by civic authorities, were a secondary gift we can all enjoy today.

The circumstances of his murder were a tawdry

conclusion to a life of vision and consequence. He may rest in an unmarked grave in the land of his birth, but surely his spirit remains in Victoria and the beautiful monuments he helped create.

Bibliography

Barrett, Anthony A., and Liscombe, Rhodri Windsor. *Francis Rattenbury and British Columbia.* Vancouver: UBC Press, 1983.

Berton, Pierre. *Klondike.* Toronto: McClelland & Stewart, 1963.

Black, Martha Louise. *My Ninety Years.* Edited by Flo Whyard. Anchorage: Alaska Northwest Publishing Co., 1976.

Gregson, H. *A History of Victoria 1842–1970.* Victoria: Observer Publishing Co., 1970.

Jesse, F. Tennyson, ed. *Trial of Alma Victoria Rattenbury and George Percy Stoner.* Notable British Trials Series. London: W. Hodge, 1935.

Kalman, Harold. *A History of Canadian Architecture.* Volume 1. Don Mills: Oxford University Press, 1994.

Bibliography

Morgan, Murray. *One Man's Gold Rush.* Vancouver: J.J. Douglas Ltd., 1973.

Ormsby, Margaret. *British Columbia: A History.* Toronto: Macmillan, 1958.

Reksten, Terry. *Rattenbury.* Victoria: Sono Nis Press, 1978.

Satterfield, Archie. *Chilkoot Pass: Then and Now.* Anchorage: Alaska Northwest Publishing Co., 1973.

About the Author

Stan Sauerwein lives and writes in Westbank, British Columbia. A freelance writer for two decades, his articles have appeared in a variety of Canadian and US magazines and newspapers. Specializing in business subjects, he has written for both corporations and governments. He is the author of *Fintry: Lives, Loves and Dreams.*

Acknowledgments

The author acknowledges two excellent books on the life of Francis Rattenbury which provided invaluable sources for quotes contained in this book: the very readable and entertaining work by Terry Reksten, *Rattenbury*, and the scholarly architectural history provided by Anthony Barrett and Rhodri Windsor, *Francis Rattenbury and British Columbia*. In both cases, the works explored Rattenbury in enormous detail and are highly recommended. I also want to thank the staff at the Museum of Northern British Columbia in Prince Rupert for their help in tracking down facts. Thanks as well to Audrey McClellan, who matches a sharp blue pencil with patience and wit.

Photograph Credits
Cover: Reproduced courtesy of the City of Victoria Archives (PR35-800). **BC Archives**: page 39 (B-07986). **John Walls:** pages 24 and 68.

OTHER AMAZING STORIES

These titles are available wherever you buy books. If you have trouble finding the book you want, call the Altitude order desk at 1-800-957-6888, e-mail your request to: orderdesk@altitudepublishing.com or visit our Web site at www.amazingstories.ca

New AMAZING STORIES titles are published every month. If you would like more information, e-mail your name and mailing address to: amazingstories@altitudepublishing.com.